Office for One:
The Sole Proprietor's Survival Guide

Christina Hamlett

DEDICATION

To Aria and Claire,
the next generation of creative thinkers
and successful businesswomen

and

To Lucy, Chief Canine Officer,
for reminding me that walks, naps and treats
are an important part of a well balanced life

****

Cover Photograph by Michael Connors
http://www.mconnors.com

Cover Design by Christina Hamlett

Cover Layout by Agy Wilson
http://www.agywilson.com

Continuity Editing by Mark Webb

TABLE OF CONTENTS

FOREWORD

INTRODUCTION   5

THINKING OUTSIDE THE BOX AT 25 VS. 55   11

   Taking On the World
   (Ben Yennie)

   It Started With a Lemonade Stand
   (Adrianne Marie Hall)

   Fired at Fifty
   (Christine Till)

TUNING OUT THE NAYSAYERS   21

   My Life, My Rules
   (Mandy Wildman)

BACK ROOM BASICS: PROTECTING YOUR STUFF   31

   *An Interview with Attorney Matthew Tynan of Pelosi Wolf
   Effron & Spates*

CLICK AND MORTAR   43

   *From High Fashion Footwear Boutique Owner To Online
   Marketing Nerd*
   (Emilia Rossi)

   Don't Believe The Hype About Online Business
   (Magda de Berg)

BALANCE AND BOUNDARIES   55

   Wherever I Lay My Hat
   (Michelle Tupy)

   Full-Time Everything
   (Sarah O'Bryan)

Me, Myself and I (and a Dog Named Barney)
(John Churchman)

FINANCIAL CHALLENGES   65

An Interview with Joel Peterson, CEO of Pintoresco Advisors

THE ACCOUNTANT: A SOLE PROPRIETOR'S BEST   75
FRIEND

An Interview with Steven S. Tyre, CPA

FINE TUNED BUDGETS AND FINE PRINT
LEGALITIES   85

Get Your Finances in Order!
(Deirdre Morhet)

For My Eyes Only
(Isabel Green, Ph.D.)

Ensuring/Insuring Successful Outcomes
(Marti Masterson)

IF YOU BUILD IT, THEY MAY (OR MAY NOT)   99
COME

Who's Your Dream Client?
(Anthony Kirlew)

MEETS AND GREETS   109

First and Last(ing) Impressions
(Tony Wilkins)

Welcome To Your Virtual Cocktail Party
(Shari Stauch)

Event Central
(John Leo Weber)

How Not To Work a Room
(Flo Selfman)

HELP WANTED 123

Paging Alex Keaton
(Jeanette Chasworth)

The Delegation of Work
(Leanne Hoagland-Smith)

Managing Your "Away Team"
(Wendy Anderson)

THE FRUGAL MARKETER 137

The Lone Wolf
(Mindy Littman Holland)

Dollars and Sense
(Corine La Font)

Let's Give Them Something To Talk About
(Garrett Mehrguth)

*Pictures Worth A Thousand Words...But Not Costing
Thousands Of Dollars*
(Jan Dunlap)

CRACKING THE MEDIA CODE 149

Media Readiness
(Cecelia Haddad)

Perfecting the Press Kit
(Lana McAra)

A Smorgasbord of Affordable PR
(Melody Friberg)

Be Your Own Producer!
(Shari Stauch)

BE OUR GUEST 169

Reach Your Audience With Guest Blogging
(Danny Iny)

RUBICONS AND BURNOUTS 179

*How Persistence In Your Life And Business Gets You What
You Want Every Time*
(Diane Conklin)

*Lost That Loving Feeling? – 10 Tips To Help You Reignite
Your Passion For Your Business*
(Jennifer Martin)

Expect the Unexpected
(Dianne Harris)

RESOURCES 191

Books

Consultants/Businesses/Support Services

Government Entities and Business Associations

Magazines and Newsletters

CONTRIBUTOR BIOS 201

FOREWORD

Why climb the corporate ladder when you can build an elevator in your own building? - Joshua E. Leyenhorst

I frequently get asked by people who are considering opening a small business if I think it's a good idea. After all, isn't it the American dream to run your own company, set your own hours, and make decisions based on what you do and what you really enjoy?

As a small business owner, albeit one with employees, I would encourage anyone thinking about starting their own enterprise – and especially as a sole proprietor - to pursue that quest but to first think long and hard about what they will need to do to make it successful.

Here are some questions to ask yourself:

- What are your goals in life?
- Why do you believe starting your own business is the best way to meet those goals?
- Do you understand that when you start your own business, most of the work that you will be <u>required</u> to do has nothing to do with your passion, your skills, or the mission of your business? You will be responsible for everything!
- Who are you trying to serve with your business? Why is this important to you? Why is this important to them?
- Are you willing, able, and ready to sacrifice free time, family time, and an income for an indeterminate duration?
- Are you able to manage yourself? Set deadlines, meet deadlines, set goals, meet goals, and realistically measure your own success? Can you improve and grow under your OWN supervision?
- What type of business do you want - not product or service - but what type? Employees? Size? Local? International? Virtual? Why?
- Are you able to adjust your thinking, your decision making, and your business plan constantly to meet the demands of your market? Do you understand that your business is not only about you?

- Are you ready to fail A LOT? Are you ready to make MISTAKES all the time? Are you ready to spend A LOT OF MONEY? Are you ready to MAKE DECISIONS that you've never made before?
- Are you ready to learn and process information faster and more accurately than ever before?
- What is the MISSION of your business? Does this Mission inspire you enough to do this every single day, under your own guidance; and will it be strong enough to inspire employees, vendors, contractors and your customers? Is it a Mission than can be the light which leads a business to success?

Over the years I've made many presentations to kids in high school and I always ask the question, "If you sell something for a dollar, how much profit do you think you will make?" Their answers are usually in the range of 25 to 75 cents. What I point out to them is that if you're someone who has no employees on the payroll, you still have to consider your materials and equipment, overhead costs such as insurance, taxes and fees, debt repayment, etc. Even if you have minimal cost in any of these areas, you need to ask yourself, "What is my TIME worth?"

For example, let's say you take on a job that requires research as well as the production of a written document. How much time is the research going to take? How much time is the document going to take to write, edit and proofread? Even if you get these two questions right, a further question is how much time do you spend marketing the finished product and, further, did you include this in your cost?

When you start your business, you will probably work more hours than you have ever worked before. I once attended a meeting in which a representative from the Service Corps of Retired Executives (SCORE) was speaking to a group of budding entrepreneurs. He mentioned that, in the past, people have stated they wanted to start a business and work only half a day. His response was, "Okay, but you need to decide <u>which</u> twelve hours you need to spend working."

Having said this, if you are successful you will reap great rewards not only monetarily but in also learning a lot about yourself and making a difference in the lives of others Even if you are <u>not</u> successful, it can still be a rewarding experience. Just don't take any of the steps lightly!

I equate it to having a child in that it becomes a part of you and, subsequently, everything you do. Within these chapters of *Office for One,* you are provided expert resources, tips and "been there/done that" insights that will not only help you start your own business but will help you evaluate as well whether this is truly the right decision for you, your lifestyle and your financial future.

Scott G. Hauge
President/Founder
Small Business California

INTRODUCTION

"A chair is still a chair
Even when there's no one sitting there"

Burt Bacharach/Hal David
Promises, Promises (1968)

When you take a leap of faith and promise yourself to start the business of your dreams, an empty chair in an Office For One symbolizes two things.

The first is that you're now the captain of a new ship about to take its maiden voyage. There's no boss looking over your shoulder, no cubicle mates to gossip with at the water cooler, no time-clock to punch. You're free to chart your own course, drop anchor in any port of call that looks interesting, and decide how to spend whatever treasure you might discover along the way. That chair represents an end to over-stuffed committees, snore-fest staff meetings, annual performance reviews, and snarky office politics…and the beginning of a fasten-your-seatbelt adventure in which every risk and every reward will carry your signature style. It's the place where you'll imagine, you'll plan, you'll create, you'll reinvent. If it's comfortable, you may even take occasional naps in it with no worries of censure or interruptions, for you'll know that you – and you alone – have earned the right to sit there as long as you want.

Not every aspect of an empty chair is quite so welcoming, however. Depending on how many years you spent being an employee of someone else, there's a possibility that all of the things you couldn't wait to get away from are among the first things you'll miss when you become your own boss. The organizational structure, rules and deadlines that previously allowed you to multi-task with gusto from 9 to 5 are no longer part of your daily routine, a dramatic shift that – in the absence of self-discipline – can lead to binge-watching multiple seasons of TV shows, playing computer games, and spending way too much time on email. The lines between your professional life and your personal life can become blurred, especially if they co-exist 24/7 under the same roof. Calling in sick to play hooky isn't what it used to be, either, nor can you delegate tasks and errands when you're caught in a crunch.

As the saying goes, it's lonely at the top. It can be incredibly lonely sitting in that chair, too.

*****

The idea for this book came from the observation that although there was a bounty of titles on the market targeted to small businesses, none of them were addressing the unique wants and needs of the smallest business of all – the sole proprietor. Likewise, my colleagues and I were spending lots of money – and valuable time – on small business workshops which assume that the participants have actual employees. Topics such as "How to Motivate Your Team" (uh – what team?), "How To Choose the Best Payroll Company" (uh – I'm only paying one person: Me) and "How to Resolve Personnel Conflicts" (uh – me, myself and I get along quite well) didn't apply to the day-to-day challenges of managing a micro-enterprise.

To add insult to injury, many chambers of commerce across the country don't have a "sole proprietor" designation when one applies for membership to take advantage of local resource and networking opportunities. If you choose not to label yourself as a small business owner, the only other choices are "Work From Home" (i.e., telemarketing, recruiting, affiliate sales, bookkeeping, or being a virtual assistant to a remote employer) or "Home-Based" (i.e., arts/crafts, piano lessons, daycare for children or pets).

But what if you're an independent consultant,

decorator, writer, graphic designer, personal trainer, tax preparer, therapist or videographer? Clearly you don't fit into either of these chamber of commerce categories. Further, "home-based" often carries a negative connotation that you're more of a casual hobbyist than a driven professional or that you're woefully unsociable and can't function in a "normal" workplace like everyone else.

Let's face facts. Not every personality, lifestyle or biological rhythm is well suited to conventional 9-5 employment. Maybe you're someone who hits your best stride after the sun goes down, loses all track of time when you're energized doing something you love, or just hates the tedium of always having to get group consensus before moving forward on even the most minor decisions. Maybe you're someone who yearns for a portable career that can go anywhere in the world that you do, or one that allows you to ditch a stressful daily commute, work from the comfort of your own house and spend more time with those you love. Maybe you even see this leap of faith as a preemptive measure stemming from the angst of becoming jobless as a result of your employer downsizing, outsourcing, merging or going bankrupt.

While enrollment in entrepreneurship programs is currently high among millennials, the youthful enthusiasm to start a business from scratch is often tempered by risk aversion, corporate "Goliath" consolidations that make small start-ups nervous about competition, shifts in government regulation and yes, the ever-daunting onus of repaying student loans. For entrepreneurs whose college years are long past, there are considerations such as raising offspring, supporting their educational pursuits, managing a mortgage, and staying healthy – all of which impact one's ability to consistently bring in an income that will keep the bills paid.

Still reading? Good. Let's start with some critical questions to determine if you're truly up for the challenges ahead.

- What are the top three reasons you want to be in business for yourself? (Be honest!)
- What are the top three skill sets you possess that you believe best position you to be your own boss?
- Will your proposed business sell products, services or a combination?

- Who do you believe needs these products and services (and why)?
- Who else is already delivering these products and services and what do you think distinguishes your own approach as an up-and-coming competitor?
- Is your education and work experience sufficient to run this business or do you need to take classes or acquire special licenses/certifications/permits?
- Could your business idea initially be launched part-time to test the waters?
- Is your business concept sustainable?
- What is your exit strategy?

The last question in this list pertains just as much to what you're going to do if things don't work out (looking for a new job or trying to go back to your old one) as it does to planning for your company's future growth. Will it one day reach the point that you'll want to diversify your product line? Incorporate new services? Enter into a partnership? Start hiring employees? Cross "starting my own business" off your bucket list and go do something completely different?

One of the elements that many sole proprietors fail to take into consideration is whether their business model is realistically "scalable" to their personal investment of time and interest. As an example, my husband and I many years ago discovered a charming shop along the Royal Mile in Edinburgh that was run by a woman who loved to knit. The shelves and racks were filled with custom designed sweaters, scarves, caps and gloves that she had made entirely by herself. She related how many customers told her that she could reach more people if she just set up a website and sold her merchandise online. While she had no doubts her designs would find an eager following, she confessed to us in her thick Scottish brogue that she only had but the ten fingers and unless she could teach her toes to "wheedle the needles," there'd be no way she could keep up with the demand.

She also pointed out that a lot of the joy she derived from her craft was simply talking to the people who came in to buy something from her.

And that brings us to what is the final and most important aspect of this bold new journey you're contemplating. If you become so preoccupied with your own screen – a definite hazard if your sole proprietorship exists only in cyberspace – you can all too easily forget how to promote the necessary growth levels that come from in-person connectivity.

So get out of that chair. Have lunch with a friend. Take a long walk with the dog. Go see what's new and going on in a world that keeps spinning whether you're working or not.

Don't worry. Your chair will still be waiting for you when you get back.

Christina Hamlett
Editor

THINKING OUTSIDE THE BOX
AT 25 vs. 55

The very existence of flamethrowers proves that sometime, somewhere, someone said to themselves, "You know, I want to set those people over there on fire, but I'm just not close enough to get the job done." – George Carlin

Among the overused metaphors about progress, invention, and career advancement is the one about expanding your mental margins by "thinking outside the box." While it's certainly true that unconventional approaches throughout history have given us a broad range of time and labor-saving devices, the memo that way too many people seem to miss is the fact that before you can start breaking the rules, you have to first learn what those rules actually are.

In other words, have you ever spent time *in* that box you're trying to bust out of?

In an earlier day, it was called "paying your dues" and "learning the ropes." It was about listening to mentors, participating in hands-on training, making trial-and-error mistakes, and identifying the academic credentials and skill sets required to climb the ladder and achieve success. That was then. This is now. A now in which, sadly, an entire generation feels entitled to bypass all of the recommended reading, placement exams and entry-level jobs and not only be installed at the top of the class but also on the very top rung of that competitive corporate ladder.

While more opportunities exist today than yesterday for free spirits to chase whatever dreams beckon and become solo entrepreneurs, there's a clear and disconcerting disconnect in appreciating the efforts of the dreamers – and hard work – that all came before and made those opportunities possible.

Whether it's the intern who expects a corner office on her first day, the new busboy who tells the chef, "Cooking doesn't look that hard – why not just let me take a spin in the kitchen tonight?" or the aspiring screenwriter who eschews the strict industry protocols of formatting, there's an escalating mindset of individuals wanting to reinvent a wheel just for the sake of reinvention, of being different, of making a statement. There are also those who say, "Working for myself is way easier than looking for a job." In reality, though, you're not working just for yourself; you're working to fill the needs of all the customers you haven't met yet. You may be the boss of your own business but guess what? Those customers are going to be the boss of <u>you</u>.

If it's your dream to design a more efficient car, to improve health care delivery, or to write a boffo movie plot no one has ever seen before, we say, "Bravo!" Before you take that daring flight of fancy, however, you first have to study existing vehicles inside-out, identify deficiencies in current health care programs, and watch a century worth of films before you proclaim that your premise of a cute extraterrestrial getting left behind by the mother ship and making friends with kids in suburbia is an original concept that people should pay attention to. In a nutshell, knowing what has already been done before is critical if you plan to lay any claim as to how to do it better.

Just as critical to this process is having a keen sense of your own capabilities, self-confidence and perseverance. Human beings – just like the businesses they launch – are quintessential works-in-progress that need to be able to respond to a broad spectrum of challenges along the road to self-sufficiency and a sustainable income.

There's also only so much time you can spend in a wishful state of always waiting for a celestial sign that it's exactly the right moment to turn your vision into an action plan. "The world needs dreamers and the world needs doers," wrote author Sarah Ban Breathnach (*Simple Abundance*), "but above all, the world needs dreamers who do."

This is your wake-up call. Are you ready to answer it?
*****

TAKING ON THE WORLD

Ben Yennie, who launched his first company while still in college, is Co-Founder of Producer Foundry and Founder/CEO of Ben Yennie and Associates LLC, an independent producers representation company.

So, you're thinking about starting your own business straight out of college? First of all, I congratulate you; you're part of a rare breed. You don't want to get a job and let your employer control every aspect of your livelihood. You've taken one of the only paths towards upward mobility in our current socio-economic environment. The "safer" option most of your friends and classmates will take is certainly easier, but when you enter the system of working a 9-5 job your employer essentially takes your time and your work and all you get is your salary. You don't participate in the profits of the company that your blood, sweat, and tears contribute to. By starting a business, you've taken the scary first step to truly controlling your destiny. You should revel in it and be proud of yourself.

That said, you have an exceedingly difficult road ahead of you. For the first few years, you'll be working longer hours for less pay than your friends who took the easy road. Thanks to social media, you'll see them hitting fun milestones with new cars and other new toys while everything you have flows into your business. It's hard to not get jealous, and you'll often wonder why you've chosen this path. If you succeed, however, the rewards are truly phenomenal and something money just can't buy.

If you're like me, there was never really a choice. You were born for this. You crave an independence that only entrepreneurship can bring. People like you built this country. People not content to just get a job. People building something greater than themselves. No matter how you do it, building a business is difficult. However, there are a few key things I've learned that I can pass on to you to make it easier.

The first and most important thing is that any business lives and dies by the relationships it fosters. Not only relationships with your customers, but also with your suppliers and partners. You need to foster good and productive relationships with everyone you do business with. People will always remember the way you do business, so you need to make sure you do it in a way that makes people want to do business with you.

Always go into a business deal looking to help both parties come off better at the end of the deal. If you always do an honest and fair deal, word will spread and it will help you build more relationships. Never try to get the best deal you can at the expense of the other person. If the person you're doing business with is serious, they'll be looking to do the same. If they're looking to get the best deal they can at your expense, then they're not serious and certainly not the type of person you want to do business with. This is true not only for business relationships outside your company, but within it as well. Be careful who you choose to partner with; if they're not willing to pull their weight, the business is doomed to fail. I tell you this from personal experience and sincerely hope you avoid my mistakes.

Second, find something you're good at, and love doing. There's a good chance you'll spend 60 hours a week doing this, so you've got to enjoy it! It's better to do one thing really well than five things only all right. You need to make sure you've got something nobody else does.

Specialization can really help you here. I have lots of friends who are graphic designers. Most of them have day jobs to pay the bills because they can't find enough work. However, I have one friend who's a graphic designer specializing in designing presentations. Not only is it his primary source of income, he doesn't even need to look for clients anymore. He's been doing it long enough and has a good enough reputation that his clients find him.

I started out in a similar situation: I was trying to start a production company. I discovered I was excellent at figuring out finance and distribution for a project but didn't have the patience necessary to make the film. There are plenty of filmmakers who can write and produce a better movie than I can. I realized I was far better off focusing on helping people find distribution than continuing to struggle in making projects. I found a niche in connecting people to distributors and helping filmmakers get the best deal possible. There are a whole lot of filmmakers making movies already, but there aren't enough people who understand the process of distribution and monetization. I've found more success doing this than I ever did in making films. Luckily for me, this is also my favorite part of the process.

Whatever you do, find your niche. Figure out a way you can do what you love and still find customers. My graphics designer friend may not be doing the fantastic artwork he originally went to school for - and I may not be making movies as I trained to in film school - but we're both doing something we love in highly competitive industries.

The third and final piece of advice I can give you is that in order to succeed in business, you need to believe in yourself. If you don't believe in yourself, no one else will. You've got to stand up for what's right for your company and what's fair. If you let yourself be taken advantage of, there's no shortage of people who will do so. Just because you're young doesn't mean you don't know what you're doing, so have confidence.

This is a double-edged sword, however. Self-confidence is necessary for success but excessive ego will destroy you. Be proud of your accomplishments but never boast about things you haven't done. It's easy to get a big head, especially in your 20's. If you go in acting like you know everything, the assumption will be that you're full of it. And honestly, if you go in with that attitude, you probably are. It's okay, we've all been there. Just remember: people with decades of experience often don't know everything, either.

The biggest thing that professionals know that amateurs don't is what they don't know. If you go into a meeting and you don't know the answer to a question, don't lie. Own the fact that you don't know it, and say that you'll find out. On a similar note, while it's important to take pride and ownership in your accomplishments, you need to take equal ownership of your mistakes. This is your company. The buck stops with you. You can't blame someone else for everything that goes wrong. Owning both your successes and failures allows you to build the self-confidence and self-awareness you need to be successful entrepreneur.

While the road ahead of you is difficult and daunting, don't be afraid. You have taken the first steps to building a truly independent life. Take advantage of it and build something to be proud of. It's not easy; but then, nothing worth having ever is.

*****

IT STARTED WITH A LEMONADE STAND

Adrianne Marie Hall is founder/owner of Anthurium Publishing LLC – an independent endeavor honed from 30+ years in business management, customer service and organizational development.

Those of us who are entrepreneurs understand the concept of creating value out of an idea. We serendipitously discover untapped or under-tapped services or products then set about trying to build a business around them hoping that others - whom we call clients and customers - will want to pay us for that service or product. Remembering when that entrepreneur bug bit us for the first time can be a wonderful trip down memory lane. I remember when the bug first bit me which was fifty years ago.

It was the summer that I was five years old and I wanted to set up a lemonade stand outside of my childhood home. When I asked my mom about it, she told me "no" because I was too little. So I did what any other little girl would do in that situation. I asked my dad who just so happened to be a successful business man.

From Dad's perspective I wanted to start a business. So instead of giving me a "yes" or "no" answer, he took me by the hand and walked me out to our lemon tree and showed me that I was not yet tall enough to reach the lowest hanging lemons. He explained that at the moment gaining access to my available supply of product would be extremely difficult. Then he walked me to the front yard of our property and showed me how our house sat at a busy intersection with virtually no foot traffic. He explained that without foot traffic I would need to find some other way to reach customers or I might have a hard time selling lemonade.

Then he walked me back to the kitchen and asked me if I knew how to make lemonade. When I acknowledged that I didn't, he explained how preparation was the one thing that could get in the way of successfully accomplishing just about anything in life from getting A's in school to running a lemonade stand. Thanks to my dad's wisdom, at five years old I learned the value of preparation. That lesson has served me well for five decades.

I never gave much thought into opening a lemonade stand after that day; however, when summer came around the next year I was a lot taller and could reach beyond the lowest hanging lemons on our tree. By the end of that summer I could stir up an amazing pitcher of lemonade, and brew up an outstanding batch of sweet tea with lemon all in a matter of minutes.

In my teens I discovered a love for creative writing which quickly grew into a desire to become a published author. I went on to college and earned a degree in psychology. Started working, then started a family. Although raising my children was my greatest priority, during that time I continued to write poetry, short stories and even completed two novels. It wasn't until after my children were grown that I achieved my first publishing goal with my novel *THRESHOLDS* in January 2013.

Going through the publishing process was the deciding factor in my pushing forward and achieving yet another goal to start my own publishing company. By May of 2013 Anthurium Publishing LLC was launched. Now clearly I did not wake up one morning and say, "I think I'm going to start my own publishing company today." No, it actually took several years from the beginning of my thought process to finally taking that entrepreneurial leap.

Before becoming a published author, for years I had been diligently investing time educating myself about the publishing industry. I attending workshops, talked to publishing professional and authors, I did countless hours of research, and read books and collected as much information as I could find on everything related to publishing.

Thanks to my dad, I understood very early in life that preparation for business ownership had many layers. Of course it was necessary that I learned as much as possible about *any* potential entrepreneurial endeavor before jumping into it. I also felt it necessary to invest time into strengthening my interpersonal skills.

While raising my children I went back to college and earned a degree in multimedia technology which actually complemented my psychology degree. I turned a jewelry making hobby into a handcrafted product called Beadie Beads BookJewelry™ which I have been direct selling to customers for fifteen years. Over thirty years I built a career working in the for-profit and nonprofit sectors honing my expertise in office management, bookkeeping, customer services, and business administration. Educational opportunities are everywhere.

Becoming a published author was like finally being tall enough to reach past the lowest hanging lemons on the tree. It was also a necessary step for me to take so that I would understand how going through the publishing process felt from a client's perspective before moving forward with my own business. Experience is actually the best teacher.

My advice to anyone thinking about business ownership is not to rush and jump into an entrepreneurial endeavor without fully understanding it. Next to parenting, it will be one of the most rewarding, validating, exhilarating, frustrating, and difficult things that anyone might choose to do. It comes with a multitude of perks, but it also comes with a multitude of responsibilities. When running a business solo, everything from paying the bills to emptying the trash is your responsibility. It helps to be organized, conscious of time management, and possess a seriously strong work ethic.

Set boundaries with anyone who does not respect that just because you work from home doesn't mean you're not busy working. During your business hours, be careful not to get caught up in non-moneymaking interruptions. Depending on your business, an hour gossiping with a friend can result in an hour of lost revenue. Expect no one to respect your business if you don't respect it yourself.

Even if it is a lemonade stand.

*****

FIRED AT FIFTY

Entrepreneur and "Marketing Mentress" Christine Till is the author of "Fired at Fifty: Stop Looking For Work and Discover What You Were Meant To Do."

January 4, 2011, I walked into the office of a senior care company where I had been working as the Director of Sales and Marketing for the past 2.5 years. I had my marketing plan for the New Year in hand and was ready to "hit the ground running." Upon entering the office, I was immediately invited into the conference room. This was not good! You know the feeling you get when you're invited into the conference room by your boss and you don't even have your coat off yet? Well, this was it.

I sat there listening to my boss expound upon all my attributes, like how hard a worker I was and that is why he kept me on for so long. My mind wandered to thoughts of "I was number 7 in a long line of Sales Directors for this company, and the company had only been in business for 7 years!" I also remembered I had brought the company sales up by an additional $22K a month within the first six months of working there.

But my boss had failed to remember all of that.

His voice faded into oblivion as I struggled to choke back the tears and squash the huge lump in my stomach. That was it. I was fired! No other words for it. Oh people say they are pink-slipped, downsized, outsized, side-stepped, but if your company does not have another position for you, you are quite simply just FIRED.

Well, I couldn't get my things packed up and my desk cleaned out fast enough. Then I was driven home because, yes, of course, the company car was no longer mine to drive.

Once in the sanctuary of my own home, the floodgates opened and the pity party was on. There were all the negative thoughts of what could I have done better and how could I have "mucked up" so badly. You can imagine the self-talk I put myself through. Definitely not good thoughts.

Have you found yourself in a similar position in your life? How did you feel? What did you do? I've met many people who have found themselves in this same type of situation, whether they have been fired, or they have quit because they couldn't stand to work for their boss any longer. When they tried to find work again, the prospects were bleak to say the least.

Here's what I did.

After a few days, I pulled myself up from the doldrums of despair and decided to start looking for work. I sent out myriad resumes and cover letters. There were so many, I lost count. Then I started receiving responses to my applications. I had four responses and one job offer for ten dollars an hour! I just sat there stunned. It was all I could do to muster a polite, "I'll think about it and let you know."

Once back in my own car, the floodgates opened once again. How was I ever going to pay the mortgage and car payments, let alone feed my family on ten dollars an hour? I would have to work three full-time jobs at this rate if I was ever going to get ahead. Hmmm…no sleep for me! More flooding.

You would think after all these years of education, experience, wisdom and knowledge that I was worth a whole lot more than ten dollars an hour. If other people were working for this kind of income, how on earth were they surviving?

Thank goodness my hubby had a job to sustain us…sort of. We really needed two incomes in order to survive.

The statistics say that 72% of married women are working these days, but personally, I think it's much higher than that. It's probably more like 85% of married women are working. It is all in how you define "work". Many women are stay-at-home moms but they have home-based businesses/jobs to help bring in extra income for the family. That was what I did all my life when my children were young, but I digress.

Back to my dilemma of being out of work. During my process of searching, I discovered that many companies make it a policy not to hire anyone close to 50 years of age. Here's why: (1) Companies feel they cannot afford to pay the higher wages that a more mature and experienced person would command; (2) Companies know that older employees tend to use the extended medical services plan more and this drives their monthly premiums up; (3) Companies want to avoid paying retirement pensions or severance fees.

Many companies feel that if they find a "legitimate" reason to let the older employees go from their jobs long before these employees reach the age of 60, they cannot be accused of dodging any retirement pensions or severance packages.

What was I to do next? Being offered only ten dollars an hour made me decide I needed to find my strengths and market myself.

If you find yourself in this same position, there are five key things you need to do as soon as possible to create an action plan:

1. What are your strengths? Make a list of all the things you have done and your experience. As you review this list, decide which ones are your best strengths.
2. Decide which strengths you can sell in the marketplace today.
3. Do you need some additional training in order to market your chosen strengths? Research the availability of classes and workshops.
4. Find out where you can get free coaching/mentoring to help you through this transition.
5. Where do you want to be five to ten years down the road? What will it take to get there?

I'll tell you a secret…I was actually 61 when I was fired. As a result, I discovered what I was truly "meant to do". What were *you* "meant to do"? There's no time like now to go find out.

TUNING OUT THE NAYSAYERS

History has given us no shortage of dreamers whose friends and foes were probably quick to say, "I told you so!" whenever one's defiance of convention resulted in fizzles, flops and failures.

- The eighth time was the charm for R. H. Macy after his first seven businesses went belly-up.
- As a youth, F. W. Woolworth wasn't allowed to wait on dry goods customers at his first job because his boss said he didn't have any sense.
- Fledgling author Dr. Seuss was rejected by 27 publishers before someone finally decided to give his stories a chance. Jack London tops that rejection count with 600 "no's" before he got *his* first "yes."
- Henry Ford went broke five times before launching a car company that finally found success.
- Elvis Presley was fired after his debut performance and advised to go back to driving a truck.
- Long before he gave the world The Happiest Place on Earth, Walt Disney was fired by a newspaper editor who told him he lacked imagination and good ideas.
- The Wright Brothers went through years of failed prototypes until they came up with a model that literally got off the ground.
- Vincent Van Gogh sold only one painting during his lifetime and yet kept at it because – well, he really liked to paint.

The lesson here is that if any of the visionaries on this list had caved to the pressures of the bliss-blowers and shelved their dreams in deference to a well-lit, safe and predictable path of ordinariness, what a loss it would have been to the generations that followed.

So it is as well with aspiring sole proprietors. If you have the aptitude for your chosen field – coupled with the patience and ambition to learn how to make your ideas work in a commercial context – the world is truly an oyster of your own making.

Just make sure your shell has enough layers of insulation to drown out the noise of everyone pounding on it and saying you should be making something else.

*****

MY LIFE, MY RULES

Mandy Wildman has worked with soul-centered solopreneurs for more than 15 years and is known as 'the slightly psychic success coach' because her spirit guides offer assistance during mentoring sessions.

You're excited about your business idea. You're so excited that you can't wait to share it with everyone you know – especially your family and friends.

You would think that when you're excited about something as big and important as the brand new business you're starting, that everyone you tell about it – especially those close to you – would be thrilled for you. And some will be, but it's horribly disappointing when instead of being supportive and encouraging, the people you care most about act as if you just announced that you were going dumpster diving for dinner and would they like to join you.

What is it that makes some people react less than enthusiastically when you tell them you're going to start your own business? Let's analyze this for a moment so that we understand where it's coming from and how to manage it.

Other People's Reactions

An example of a disappointing reaction to your big announcement might be:

You: "I'm so excited – I'm finally going to start that business I told you about!"
Them: "Really? Why? Did you lose your job?"
You: "Noooo, I'm *quitting* my job!"
Them (gasping): "Why would you want to quit a perfectly good job to do something risky like that?"

Another fairly common example:

You: "I'm thinking about turning my passion into a business."
Them: "How are you going to do that with two kids

and a full-time job?"

You: "I'll do it in the evenings and weekends in my spare time."

Them: "Who's going to watch the kids?"

You: "Well – their dad can help out, and my mom said she'd watch them for me sometimes..."

Them: "Won't that be hard on the kids? I mean they won't get to spend as much time with you, and it'll put a strain on your mom, and isn't that why their dad left you – because you weren't giving him what he said he needed, *(blah, blah, blah)*?"

By this time you're feeling guilty, nervous, unsure, doubtful and ready to re-evaluate the whole idea. And there goes another five years of your life while you stop to do everything you can to make other people happy. Newsflash – it's impossible (and not your job – *ever*) to 'make other people happy.' The only person who can ever decide whether they are happy or not is THEM, and if they're hinging *their* happiness on what *you* do or don't do, then they are *giving away their personal power.*

Let's flip this around: If you're dependent upon how other people react for *you* to feel good, then YOU are giving away *your* power, do you see?

When asked for advice, the first thing I tell aspiring solopreneurs is this: What other people think of you is none of your business. Why? Because the whole essence of solopreneurism revolves around creativity, independence and freedom. All things that typically are shunned, mocked or frowned upon in what is basically a "slave-to-the-corporate-giants" societal structure.

Here are three reasons that people will react negatively to the news that you are starting your own business: (1) They are envious, (2) They are fearful, or (3) They are intentionally trying to make nothing of your dreams. We'll take them one by one.

Negative comments are often based on Envy. That's right. Here you come, all enthusiastic, announcing that you're breaking free. You're saying 'no!' to the status quo. You're going to be having fun, doing what you adore, every single day. No more 9-5pm for you (as a business owner you'll work much longer hours than that! For example, I am writing this on a beautiful Sunday afternoon while my husband and three kids are out on a fun trip. I'm good with it, and so are they).

So your act of optimistic heroism just flies in the face of everything these naysayers have been taught, seen or believed. All that happiness and success is for other people, not them. And (in their mind) not you, either.

Another reason for negativity is Fear. This is common with parents, who care about you deeply and are concerned that you'll get into a situation that they can't help you with. Coming from a different generation and having lots of 'life experience' under their belt, they see the downside in everything – it's part of a parent's job to be protective and to do all they can to stop you from taking what they see as unnecessary risks.

You'll hear ugly phrases such as, "financial suicide" or "throwing away everything you've worked for," and if things get heated, someone is bound to trot out that tired old downer: "80% of all small businesses fail within the first two years." While it's a good idea to be respectful, it's just as important to be ready for this type of conversation by gently explaining that just because you can't staticize things like "happiness," "satisfaction," or "fulfillment" doesn't mean that they aren't as important as what statisticians and financial analysts may deem to be 'successful.' If they argue that you're wasting your education and/or experience you can let them know that your education and experience are part of what prepared you for this adventure. If they pester you about squandering your security, offer them this Helen Keller quote: "Security is mostly a superstition. Avoiding danger is no safer in the long run than outright experience. Life is either a daring adventure or nothing."

The courage you show when you follow your dreams despite what society dictates challenges the fearful person's comfort zone and that makes them uncomfortable. I personally believe comfort zones were meant to be re-defined regularly. It's more fun that way. And if you're reading this, I think you believe that, too.

The third source of negativity comes from that very small percentage of people who are committed to being destructive and vindictive and making dust of your dreams. I call them The Doom Squad. They spend their lives dedicated to providing victims with their vicious put-downs masquerading as 'helpful advice.' Clearly they don't deserve your time or attention, so just shut them down and walk away.

It's that simple.

It's up to you to determine which of the three types of people you're dealing with and handle them accordingly. Ultimately, you have to decide how important their opinions are to you. It comes down to this: Are you alive? Check. Are you challenging yourself? Check. Are you feeling happy and excited for the future? Check. Good, then carry on.

Being Attached to Specific Outcomes

It's easy to get caught up in being attached to specific outcomes, especially when it comes to doing something that is heart-centered like starting your own business. Certainly when people you respect offer up advice about what their idea of a 'proper outcome' would be for your business, it's very easy to get sucked in to that mindset.

Example:

Them: "You have to have a business plan that is 3-5 inches thick and then you have to convince a lending institution to give you a loan to get you going. Otherwise you'll never make it."

You listen to this and say to yourself, *"I'm going to present my 3-5 inch thick business plan to these 3 lenders and if they say yes I'm going to be so happy!"* This becomes a recipe for disaster, here's how: All three (and maybe more) potential lenders turn down your request for a loan, giving you various reasons for why they don't think you are a good risk. You are horribly disappointed.

You: *"They all said 'no'. They said I had to have collateral and I don't have any. I'm so disappointed. Maybe I wasn't meant to own my own business. I'll probably never make it. Maybe I should just look for a job."*

You see what happened there? On the advice of a friend (or even an 'expert') you decided that your success hinged on getting a start-up loan. You were attached to that specific outcome, and when it didn't turn out the way you expected, you felt deflated and began to question whether starting your own business was a good idea.

But what about starting with what you already have, even if it doesn't seem like much? What about 'bootstrapping' it with resources you already have access to? (If you think about it, you *do* have resources) What about tweaking your idea a tad or finding a different route? A little research (with an upbeat attitude) will turn up thousands of stories of people who built thriving businesses from scratch. One millionaire I know started her business from the trunk of her car because she was homeless at the time!

You have to allow the Universe do its job by being open to different possible outcomes because the danger is, when an exact expected outcome is not met, the mental peanut gallery can get very, very noisy.

Protecting Yourself from The Peanut Gallery

We talked earlier about the negative reactions of those around you, but now let's talk about *why* their opinions would even affect you.

Their negativity affects you because their limiting beliefs are feeding into yours. You know what I'm talking about - that gang of naysayers inside your head. I refer to them as The Peanut Gallery. This is a collective term for those 'helpful' voices in your head (don't even try to pretend they don't exist!) that are so willing to serve up those almost true-sounding but grim thoughts that make you think less of yourself and encourage you to abandon your dreams to dust before they have a chance to take wing. They are the ugly thoughts and critical comments that you believe are coming from YOU (they're not). Let me explain.

When you're feeling down, anxious, fearful, resentful and discouraged, that's not the real you. That's The Peanut Gallery at work. Those negative thoughts work hard at getting you to believe they represent the truth – but they don't.

You are everything that is good, funny, happy and positive. The real *you* is brilliant, generous, excited and creative. The real *you* loves people and nature and life. The real *you* knows things intuitively, and can tell the difference between what will be good for you, and what won't.

The thing to remember is, they are not the boss of you - YOU are. You are in the driver's seat and you get to say what's true for you and what isn't. The trick is to replace any negative thought with something more positive. Just flip it around. Here are some examples (yes, I love giving examples):

"What if I fail at business?" becomes "What if I don't? My business could turn out to be fabulously successful."

"What if I don't make enough money?" becomes "I could always do something else part-time to make the money I need while I'm building my new business."

"What if I'm not spending as much time with my family? Will that make me a bad parent/spouse?" becomes "I'll be a better parent/spouse if I'm feeling happy and productive – the time we do spend together will be more fun."

Are you getting the idea? You really have to master this kind of thinking to get the most out of anything you do in life, so to be absolutely sure you've got this, read on.

Sanity Guidelines

So just for safety's sake (because it would make me seriously sad if you gave up your dreams on account of a few jealous comments and a couple of nagging head voices), we're going to lay out some guidelines that you can apply when embarking on the adventure of creating an awesome life and going against the advice of seemingly well-meaning people:

1.   Humans have opinions. Plenty of them. And a lot of human opinions will be downright false or at least will not be relevant to you and your life.

2.   An opinion is a belief, and a belief is something you think is true.

3.   A *limiting belief* is a negative thought that you *think* is true, but then when you really, really think about it, it's not.

4.   If something feels 'not right' to you - no matter where or who it's coming from – you can probably trace it back to a *human opinion* that is false or not relevant to you. Even if it's yours.

5.   If an opinion is being shoved down your throat it is much more likely to be false or irrelevant to you and your life. Even when it's you who are doing the shoving. (*Especially* when it's you who are doing the shoving. Can you think of examples?)

6.   The only things that are really, really true are those things that *feel* really, really true to YOU.

7.   You'll have a really hard time attracting money and success (not to mention the joy and fulfillment parts) if you don't know and apply this stuff.

There are no exceptions to these guidelines. Really.

Really, REALLY. So from now on, whenever you hear something that sounds a bit *off* to you, I recommend you stop, think, and decide whether that's really true for you or not. Some common examples of human opinion are:

- "Business is business." (What does that even mean? Sounds like a justification for doing something unethical.)
- "You can't always get what you want." (...sang Mick Jagger, now in his fifth decade of rock stardom.)
- "Seeing is believing." (Yes, and so is *knowing*.)
- "Everything will always come out all right in the end." (Actually, that's a good one. Keep that one; it might come in handy.)

Defensive Thought Strategies

You probably already know that we are living in an attraction-based Universe. But just in case you don't, here are the basics:

It's a fact that whenever you think a thought, more thoughts just like it are attracted to it like a magnet. So if you think one negative, self-limiting thought, other similar thoughts will start pouring in from the ever-obliging peanut gallery.

Whenever you're feeling discouraged about something you were previously excited about, chances are (depending on the circumstances) you're listening to The Peanut Gallery and talking yourself out of doing something daring, brave or fun.

The trick to this is to make sure you focus on thinking thoughts that make you feel good. Any time things in your life start looking funky (you know, because you're not feeling so good), your immediate defensive strategy should be to catch yourself and then work to find a thought that makes you feel better. And then find another one and another one until you are feeling pretty good or even great. That's it, that's the whole drill.

This takes some dedication and practice (it's not taught in schools) but really, there's nothing more important for you to do than just this over and over again; constantly finding better thoughts to think, and focusing on the things and people you love and the experiences you'd like to have. These better thoughts will act like magnets to attract more 'better thoughts' to come to you, which will in turn inspire you to take action to help these great thoughts become the actual experiences of your life.

Do this consistently and pretty soon you'll have all kinds of exciting opportunities and unexpected miracles presenting themselves for you to consider. And, as if by magic, the naysayers will begin to change their tune or simply go away, and your true supporters and cheerleaders will start to appear in your experience. I am one of them, and I want to thank you for reading this and sincerely wish you the best of luck with your beautiful (ad)venture.

BACK ROOM BASICS:
PROTECTING YOUR STUFF

"Experience," wrote Oscar Wilde, "is simply the name we give our mistakes." When you're starting a business from the ground up, it's a certainty there will be plenty of mistakes made along the way. Mistakes that stem from not knowing what you needed to know, not knowing that what you read (or what you were told by someone else) wasn't factually accurate, and not recognizing when you have bitten off more than you can realistically chew.

Among the worst mistakes you can make are the ones that can get you in trouble with the law and potentially cost you everything that you put into your dream, including your reputation. Like preventative medicine to address a possible health risk, consulting an attorney when you first decide to set up shop is much smarter than subsequently scrambling to find someone to fix whatever damage you've done as a do-it-yourselfer.

Oftentimes, business lawyers will either have accounting credentials as well or will be able to recommend a qualified accountant for your business needs. This is an important collaboration and can clear the field of your endeavor of the many mines that are out there on issues from licenses, contracts, copyright, and intellectual property protections to the various ways in which local, state and federal taxes affect how you do business.

No matter how competent and confident you are at being a one-person show, it can't be emphasized enough that every sole proprietor needs the advice and counsel of a team of professionals. The sooner that advice is sought, the better.

*****

Matthew Tynan (Pelosi Wolf Effron & Spates) is a transactional attorney specializing in the preparation of intellectual property and corporate agreements and the protection of client copyrights and trademarks.

Q: From a legal standpoint, are certain types of business structures more beneficial to a sole proprietor than others? For instance, is a "Sole Proprietorship" better than a "Limited Liability Company"?

A: As with all things in life and law, it depends. When it comes to choosing a business entity, there are many factors to consider. For starters, a sole proprietorship ("SP") is, by definition, an unincorporated business and not an LLC, corporation or "S" corporation. In fact, if you are conducting any kind of business by yourself without forming an entity, then you will probably be considered a sole proprietorship for tax purposes. Here are some of the key (and basic) considerations:

- Formation: SPs usually don't require any formal filings unless you decide to assume a company name in which case you may have to file your assumed name or DBA with the county clerk. In New York, single member LLCs are usually more expensive to form than sole shareholder corporations and have special publication requirements, but there are fewer business formalities to worry about going forward.

- Taxation: Each entity has its own advantages and disadvantages depending on the kind of business you have, and I strongly recommend that all new business owners consult an accountant before they choose a business entity. SPs, LLCs and so-called "S" corporations are all "flow-through" businesses for tax purposes, which means that all income and deductions flow down to the owner who is taxed directly. Regular "C"-type Corporations, on the other hand, are usually taxed twice, at the corporate level on earnings and then again at the shareholder level when dividends are distributed.

- Flexibility: SPs are very flexible and owners have complete control. What's more, there are no other members, shareholders or partners to owe fiduciary obligations.

- Limited Liability: This is perhaps the most important distinction between an SP and a formal business entity. The owner of a SP is personally on the hook for all liabilities. In the case of an LLC, for example, a creditor can only reach the assets of the company and not the owner. But be careful, if the owner doesn't take care to keep his corporate and personal identity separate, a creditor may be able to "pierce the corporate veil" and hold the owner personally liable.

Q: What's an EIN and do sole proprietors need to have one to do business?

A: A EIN is an Employee Identification Number, also known as a Federal Tax Identification Number. An EIN may not be always be necessary for a SP, but applying for one is free, fast and easy, and you will definitely need one if you plan on employing anyone and a bank will most likely require your entity to have one before you open a business account. (See: http://www.irs.gov/Businesses/Small-Businesses-&-Self-Employed/How-to-Apply-for-an-EIN.)

Q: What are some of the biggest legal mistakes that small start-ups make?

A: Not planning ahead. Most of us tend to think the best of the people we do business with, especially when we are dealing with friends or family, but things can sour very quickly when money is involved and the best way to protect your business and your personal relationships is to be prepared, and the best way to be prepared is to have something in writing ahead of time. For example, a well-drafted agreement lets all the parties know their duties and obligations and provides a roadmap for what happens when things go wrong.

And when it comes to planning ahead, it is always a good idea to register your intellectual property sooner rather than later and hopefully long before someone tries to steal it (for one thing, registration is required before you can file your copyright infringement suit in court, and if you don't register in a timely fashion, you lose out on potentially lucrative statutory damages).

Q: What's the difference between a copyright, a trademark and a patent and what, exactly, is each one supposed to protect?

A: Copyright protects original works of authorship fixed in a tangible medium. Copyright is really a bundle of separate rights, including the exclusive right to copy, distribute, create derivative works, publicly perform and display your work.

Trademarks are words or symbols or other designations that identify your goods or services and distinguish them from others. A fundamental purpose of trademark protection is to prevent consumer confusion as to the source of goods or services.

Patents cover inventions that are novel, non-obvious and useful. Both copyright and patent protection have a limited duration (in most cases, copyright lasts for the life of the author plus 70 years while a utility patent, for example, can last 20 years). Trademark protection, on the other hand, can continue indefinitely so long as the goods or services are still be used in commerce.

Q: What if you only have an <u>idea</u> for a book or a company or an invention but you haven't actually implemented any of it? Is there a way you can register your plan so that no one else will steal it before you're ready to launch?

A: Ideas are often our most valuable commodity and yet they are very difficult to protect. Copyright does not cover ideas, only the original expression of those ideas. That said, writing down your idea, or expressing it in some tangible way, may make it a little harder for someone to steal it, because the would-be thief will have to be careful not to copy any of your original expression or face a copyright infringement lawsuit.

If your idea meets all the requirements for patent protection (i.e. it is novel, non-obvious, useful etc...) then patent registration with the US Patent and Trademark Office is one option—but the process can be difficult and expensive. There are some tort remedies such as common law misappropriation, and if you have made diligent efforts to keep your idea hidden, you may be able to argue that your idea is a protected trade secret—but these options are not available in every state and can be difficult to establish in a court of law. But if you want to be absolutely safe, the best route is to have a written agreement in place before you start sharing your ideas.

Q: Are there any legal drawbacks to registering your intellectual property and business creations with the government entities that handle these?

A: When you register your trademark or copyrighted work, that registration is a matter of public record and, in the case of copyright registration, a copy of your work will be deposited with the Library of Congress and made available for inspection—but accessing the work is not easy and there are fees involved. For most people, a little public exposure is a small price to pay when compared to the numerous benefits of registration.

Q: What category does a logo fall under?

A: Trademark. But if you hire someone to design a logo for your company, make sure that you have a signed written agreement stating that you own the copyright in that design or have secured the rights to use it.

Q: Let's talk about registering the name of a new company. Can you give your business the same name that someone else already has even if they're in a different city or, for that matter, live in the same city but are doing something entirely different? For instance, what if you wanted to call your hand-painted teacup business "Custom Cups" but a lingerie shop specializing in brassieres was currently using it?

A: If you decide to form a business entity like an LLC, it is more than likely that your application will be denied if you choose the same name as an existing company in your state. But even if you decide to remain a sole proprietorship and/or register your company's DBA, you may still run into trouble if your name is confusingly similar to another company's.

As a matter of trademark law, your ability to hold on to the name depends on a variety of factors including: what kind of goods or services you offer; the geographical location you do business in; and who started using the name first. For example, even if Custom Cups Brassieres has a federal trademark registration, you may still be able to use the name to sell your teacups (even in the same city) because the goods you are selling are so different that consumers are unlikely to be confused.

But beware: even if your goods or services are completely different, the owner of a well known or "famous" trademark can sue you for "diluting" the distinctive quality of their famous mark.

Q: How do you find out if a particular business name is available?

A: There are companies that will do the research for a fee but a good place to start is your local Department or Secretary of State website where you may be able to search business entity listings for free. And, of course, there is always Google.

Q: A lot of sole proprietors like to use their own name as the company ID; i.e., Rita Jones Fashions. But what if you have a fairly common name? Can someone legally prevent you from using it just because another Mary Smith or Bob White grabbed it first?

A: It would be quite difficult, but not impossible, for someone to prevent you from using your own name for your company. For one thing, personal names are generally not eligible for trademark protection because they are primarily descriptive. One exception is when the personal name is so well-known and widely advertised as the origin of a particular good or service that it acquires "secondary meaning"—*Ford* being one famous example.

Using your own name, especially if it is not very distinctive, may well put you at a disadvantage if you want to protect your brand from trademark infringement. And don't forget that New York, like most states, will reject any name that is not "distinguishable" from a previously filed company name.

Q: Does all of this apply to website domain names, too?

A: ICANN, the regulatory body that oversees the use of internet domain names, has dispute resolution procedures in place if you think you have a trademark interest in a particular domain name and someone is using your company name in bad faith. Unfortunately, most of the time, securing a domain name is a matter of first come first served.

This issue is of particular importance right now as ICANN is in the midst of introducing hundreds of new generic top level domain names (in addition to .com, .net etc.) which may well make it even harder to protect your brand online.

For those lucky enough to have a registered trademark, you can (for a fee) sign up with ICANN's Trademark Clearinghouse and get priority registration with the new domains along with notifications when someone else tries to use your trademark in a domain name.

Q: What are cybersquatters and should I be worried about them?

A: Congress enacted the Anticybersquatting Consumer Protection Act in 1999 to prevent cybersquatters—people who acquire a domain name in bad faith intending to profit from the use of someone else's trademark. The avalanche of new top level domain names may well be a potential boon if you want to expand your presence online, but it also provides new opportunities for cybersquatters, competitors and anyone else who may wish your company ill.

Q: How do you ensure that something you put on your website (i.e., original photographs or blog content) doesn't get stolen and used by someone else without your permission?

A: While I am not an expert on the various technological protections that are available such as encryption and access controls, several simple strategies do come to mind: (1) include a well-drafted Terms of Use and Privacy Policy on your website where you let users know everything on the site belongs to you and they can't use it without your permission; (2) put copyright notices at the bottom of every page and also on all your photographs/art etc.; (3) use embedded watermarks; and (4) where applicable, add trademark symbols.

Q: If you're just an office of one but have a fictitious DBA, do you have to take out any public notices in the newspaper before you can officially "open"?

A: States differ on what is required to register a fictitious DBA and, yes, you may be required to publish a DBA statement in a local newspaper. Find out what requirements may apply in your state before you start actively using a DBA.

Q: Sole proprietors that do creative things such as ghostwriting, graphic design and copyediting are engaging in projects that are labeled "Work For Hire." What's the interface in terms of copyright issues, confidentiality, non-competes, trade secrets, and who legally owns what? Are there some common mistakes that beginners make in work-for-hire arrangements? If so, how do you avoid or address them before they escalate into ugly litigious scenarios?

A: Work-made-for-hire is a much misunderstood term. Simply put, if your creations are works made for hire, then, legally speaking, you are not the "author" of those creations and you retain no copyright interest. There are two ways that something can be work-made-for-hire: (1) you create the work as an employee in the scope of your employment, or (2) you are an independent contractor and your work was specially ordered or commissioned for use in certain kinds of work such as a contribution to a collective work, movie, translation, supplementary work, compilation, or as an instructional text <u>and</u> there is a signed agreement that your work is for hire.

Work for hire is entirely a copyright issue and it has little bearing on confidentiality, non-competes or trade-secrets.

Proper work-for-hire language in independent contractor agreements will make clear that everything (all the results and proceeds of the work) are works for hire specially ordered or commissioned, tracking the statutory requirements. Two things to look out for: (1) just in case a court decides work-for-hire does not apply, make sure that the independent contractor promises to assign all his/her rights in the work; and (2) to the extent possible, have him/her waive any "moral rights" he/she might have in the work.

Q: What is the Fair Use doctrine and how can sole proprietors apply it to what they can and can't use in their printed or online materials?

A: The most important rule to remember about fair use, is that there are no hard and fast rules! For example, don't believe anyone who says if you use less than 10% of a work it is fair use. Fair use is something only decided in a court of law and is often a very fact specific determination.

So what is it? Fair use is a defense to copyright infringement and permits the use of someone else's copyrighted work under limited circumstances. Generally, if the use is for purposes of news reporting, criticism, comment, parody, scholarship, teaching or research it is likely to be fair use.

The Copyright Act has four non-exhaustive factors that courts are meant to apply to see if the use is fair: what is the purpose and character of the use? (e.g. is it commercial?); what is the nature of the copyrighted work? (e.g. is it a very creative work, is it unpublished?); the amount and substantiality of the work used? (e.g. was the use reasonable in relation to the purpose of the copying, and/or did they use the most important part of the work?); and what is the effect on the potential market for or value of the work? (e.g. will using the work have an adverse impact on future sales?).

Above all else, courts like to ask if the use of the copyrighted work was "transformative." What this means exactly is still up for debate but the general gist, as explained by the Supreme Court, is that a use is transformative if it adds a new purpose or character to the original work and alters it with new expression or meaning.

When it comes to the use of someone else's work in your printed or online materials, it is always the safest route to obtain permission first. This is especially important if you intend to use the work in a commercial context, such as marketing materials. But keep in mind that not all works are protected by copyright, and even in a commercial context, fair use may still apply. But remember, when it comes to fair use, there are no guarantees.

Q: How about dead celebrities? For instance, if someone wanted to use an image of Elvis on their business cards or a vintage video clip of Fred and Ginger on a dance lessons website, would it be permissible?

A: This is primarily a right of publicity question but don't forget that your image of Elvis may also be protected by copyright. The right of publicity, if it exists at all, is a matter of state law but the general idea is that people should be allowed some control over the use of their name and likeness for a commercial use. As you can imagine, celebrities have a strong interest in the use of their identity for commercial purposes and are often the most protective of their image.

Whether those rights survive death varies from state to state. California, for example, recognizes a post-mortem right of publicity as long as the celebrity made commercial use of his/her name/likeness, etc. during his/her lifetime. In New York, by contrast, there is no such right after death. A 2012 decision in California held that because Marilyn Monroe was domiciled in New York when she died, New York law applied, and thus her estate had no posthumous rights in the use of her image. The take-away is that, at present, there is no uniform nationwide right of publicity, so written permissions from the dead celebrity's estate is a good idea.

Q: What if a competitor tries to discredit my small business by engaging in defamation? Do I have any legal recourse?

A: To establish *defamation*, you would commonly need to prove that your competitor made a false statement about you to a third party that caused you some harm. If you happen to be a public figure, you would also need to show that your competitor acted with "actual malice." Be aware, though, that opinion is not actionable by itself—it has to be a false assertion of fact. And the truth is an absolute defense.

There are other alternative legal claims to consider: one example is the tort of *false light* (similar to defamation, but it requires the publication of highly offensive and false facts—and doesn't exist in New York!); another route is *tortious interference with contractual relations*, and/or *tortious interference with business relations* both of which require that your competitor intentionally, and often wrongfully, interfered with your deal or business relationship, and your business was damaged as a direct result.

As before, the legal requirements for these different causes of action differ from state to state. What's more, success is never guaranteed and the process can be time-consuming and expensive.

Q: What role does the Federal Trade Commission play in testimonials, endorsements and disclosures?

A: The Bureau of Consumer Protection division of the Federal Trade Commission (FTC) enforces truth-in-advertising laws with the goal of preventing harm to consumers from unfair or deceptive acts in commerce, such as advertising. A few years back, the FTC issued revised Endorsement Guides concerning the use of endorsements and testimonials in advertising. In short, they require that (1) all endorsements be truthful and not misleading, (2) if the endorser's claims about a product aren't backed up or are not typical, that has to be disclosed, and (3) any connection between the endorser and the advertiser must be fully disclosed.

Bear in mind that the Endorsement Guides are only guidelines, not law, and there is no fine for not complying with them. But if you or the advertisers *don't* follow the guides, it could result in corrective action by the FTC.

CLICK AND MORTAR

By what definition is something "real"? Take books, for instance. Between the two of us, my husband and I have enough hardcover and paperback titles that we could easily open our own bookstore or library. We also travel a lot and have no fewer than several dozen titles loaded on our respective Kindles.

The latter is a mystifying device to my beloved aunt, a former high school English teacher. When I first explained the concept to her, she asked what I did if I wanted to read an electronic book in bed. "I don't think I'd like a big computer monitor sitting on top of me," she said. To illustrate the compact nature of what a Kindle was, I took a photograph of it next to my coffee cup. This, however, confused her even more, for how could a flat little device like that hold 3,000 books at the same time? Furthermore, what happened to those books after I read them? I told her that they could either be archived indefinitely or deleted into the ether.

"But what if you want to read it a second or third time?" she asked. I could just imagine her horror that deleted books waft somewhere into outer space and are summarily blown up, never to be seen again.

I explained that there was a retrieval system to download these books back into the queue but even this didn't satisfy her. "It would be much easier to just go take it off a shelf," she said. Old books – like old friends – have always been plentiful in her life and she takes pride in knowing exactly where all of them are.

Despite my insistence that hardcover/paperback and ebooks can co-exist in the same universe, she just doesn't believe it. Accordingly, whenever I tell her that I've just finished reading a great novel, the first question she asks is whether it was a "real" book or "one of those fake ones."

As I see it, it takes just as much time for a writer to compose an 80,000 word book that's published traditionally as it does to have that book published in a digital format. The same amount of time and care goes into designing the cover art, planning a marketing platform, and acquiring reviews. Why then, should an ebook be treated as anything less real and meaningful than that same content printed on paper?

A similar argument can be made for brick-and-mortar-establishments versus those that exist entirely online. Depending on the type of product or service you're promoting, one may work much better for you and your budget than the other or, as your company grows, there may even be a hybrid version; i.e., an online catalogue where customers can view designer merchandise and a physical store where they can try items on.

"So is it a 'real' business you've set up?" people might ask you. To which you can take a page from Margery Williams' *The Velveteen Rabbit*: "Real isn't how you're made. It's a thing that happens to you. It doesn't happen all at once. You become. Once you are real, you can't become unreal again."

If you love your business with all your heart and can't imagine going to bed or waking up without thinking about it, it doesn't get any more "real" than that, no matter where or how it happens to exist in the big scheme of things.

*****

FROM HIGH FASHION FOOTWEAR BOUTIQUE OWNER TO ONLINE MARKETING NERD

Melbourne entrepreneur Emilia Rossi consults businesses on how to develop and improve their online marketing strategies.

What I've learned about the differences between operating a storefront business and one that exists in a 24/7 virtual platform could easily fill a book!

After graduating in Industrial Design at University, I decided to follow my dream of being involved in a fashion design business. So I left my day job as an Exhibition Designer to pursue that goal and make it a reality. Fortunately, I also had the financial backing and support of my mother who was my business partner at the time.

We searched for three months until we finally found what we believed was the ideal location, leasing a 70 sqm retail space. We opened our doors in April 2008 – an enterprise that would last for the next four years.

From the very first day we were heavily involved in the day-to-day operations of the business from shop design to product selection and marketing. Our storefront incorporated a high-end, luxury feel while also being inviting. The design used clean lines, minimalist furniture and lighting that showcased the high-end leather collections. Being able to create the right mood for our clientele was important. The environment we created was frequently commented on and unique to the complex (and city) we operated in.

Due to the nature of the business (selling handcrafted leather shoes and handbags) as well as trade requirements, a storefront was required. Our designs were embellished with intricate detail where the true beauty of the product could only be experienced in person by touching, smelling and trying on designs prior to purchasing them. Our research at the time further suggested a tendency by our market to research online before buying in store.

Despite all this, retrospectively I would have done things differently. I would have launched with an ecommerce store first to test the idea and, if successful, trialed further through a temporary pop up store. If the pop-up store was successful, only then would I have made the transition to a shop front which, of course, requires a far greater commitment.

When entrepreneurs make the decision to have a physical shop from which to sell their merchandise, they obviously have to ask themselves whether it's better to own or lease the building in which the shop will be located.

Our own storefront – which we leased - was located inside a large shopping mall precinct. The space we occupied was offered at a relatively reasonable price, as it was not considered a high traffic section of the shopping mall. For us, however, the location was ideal as it was positioned adjacent to a major department store, which assisted initial brand awareness and potential traffic.

In choosing a location, we were definitely mindful of accessibility. Our audience appreciated a boutique experience so we needed to ensure the store wasn't constantly overrun by mobs of people. Maintaining an aura of being a "destination boutique" was very important. Although being in a high-traffic area would have brought greater awareness to our store, it would have presented more challenges such as higher rent and theft rates. Plus, paying twice as much for rent in a high-traffic area to attract the wrong type of customer was not part of our plan!

Being new to commercial leasing presented many obstacles. You are required to have certain legal documents and checklists in place before you are deemed safe to open to the public. These documents and checklists will be different depending on which state/country you are in. Some of these checklists took up to four weeks to be finalized! Small details like this can see you officially launch and begin paying rent, only to find you cannot trade until these documents have been signed off. My advice? Make completely sure to have everything in place well before the agreed upon launch day.

I wouldn't say finding, fitting out, opening and signing a lease for a retail space is easy by any means. It's stress-inducing but critical to do your due diligence to ensure you are not stung with any nasty surprises which can cost you time and money. You must also be realistic with your expectations. For instance, our furniture for the shop was made overseas. Not the best idea, especially when you run the risk of having your furniture held up in customs and forcing you to open with a completely bare shop. I would never do that again and instead opt to have the majority of the furniture manufactured and sourced locally. The headache of having every single piece of furniture designed and brought on a ship from overseas was a nightmare!

Putting such vexations aside, I enjoyed the experience owning my own boutique. It was a pleasure to work in the business and on the business and, in many ways, it was an extension of myself. The store was exceptionally neat and tidy. People could see how passionate I was. I always made sure to pay attention to detail and enjoyed the fact I had total control of the atmosphere created in the store.

I also enjoyed that I was able to create an amazing retail experience with the music I played, the scents I used, the coffee and chocolates I served, etc. Being able to be so hands-on with the boutique and creating unique in-store events, controlling merchandising, and setting up the shop with new designs was a pleasant experience. But it did mean I had to be on my feet for many hours at a time, in contrast to an online store where most of these things can be done whilst sitting behind a screen, in the comfort of your own home.

It's also easy to become a slave to your own dream of business ownership. The fact we had to be open 7 days a week almost 365 days a year is matched only by all the hidden costs you find out about prior to the final sign-off. These include:

- Window Glass cleaning fees - The outside window had to be cleaned once a week.
- Music licenses - We had to pay an annual fee to play music in store.
- Expensive point of sale software and equipment - If you have any sort of stock, you need a point of sale system that can control your stock count as well as your customer details. This software can become quite expensive.
- Stock shrinkage – This really annoyed me; the fact that we had people stealing our stock!
- Stock take - An expensive and very stressful task. We did frequent stock takes to ensure our stock levels were as accurate as they could be. This is how we picked up most of our stock discrepancies.
- Printings costs, signage, branding, etc.
- Expensive insurance.
- Having to fix minor issues such as burnt out lights.

Putting security in place was very expensive and, to be honest, the technology available at that time for retail security was ugly and outdated. Nothing was 100% theft-proof.

I was also annoyed that I didn't have total control over my stock. I hated the idea that someone could steal my products (unlike an ecommerce store).

Maybe it was time to transition from having a storefront to an online showroom.

After four years I came to the conclusion that operating as I did was not sustainable. Storefront overheads were pricey and the time spent in the store was a lot more than we ever imagined. At times it was draining! I felt frustrated I was starting to become the "face" of the business; when I wasn't in the shop, our sales were affected. When you become too connected to your physical store – and where sales relay on your own presence - you run the risk of not being able to expand.

As nice as it is to be able to interact with your customers – which I loved – you have to be mindful that you can only sell during your store's "open" hours and that there are extra costs to maintain the appearance of the building. Every four years, for example, a storefront's internal fit-out will need to be upgraded and, after paying years of rent, you may still never own the place.

Additional obstacles continued to be flung in my path:

- Delays in new stock arriving from overseas - While other stores already had their new designs, we were always behind. No one at that stage was importing the volume we were from South America.

- Finding good people to work with and to employ - The business relied on outstanding customer service. This was hard to find but we managed to hire only the best and achieved an excellent retention rate because our staff loved working with us.

- Couldn't expand - The complex nature of the business made it extremely expensive and challenging to grow.

I think already having experienced running and operating a business made the transition a lot easier as we knew the basics already; this gave us an advantage to pursue an online business. Without having this fundamental experience and education, I think the transition would've been far more difficult. There is never a better time to be online than now. So if you are thinking of taking that step, do it!

Clearly the greatest advantage of an online enterprise is that you can work from anywhere, you have more control, and you have the ability to make changes quickly. On the other hand, you'll be dealing with spammers, online security can be difficult and expensive, and traffic can be tough to grow, especially for new brands/sites.

Thinking of wanting both a storefront *and* an online shop? My advice is to start online, experiment with a pop-op store and – if the uptake is promising – start seeking a physical address. Having both is a very powerful combination in that you have the opportunity to improve overall online conversions through enabling your customers to visit your store, touch and feel your products and get to know the brand enough prior to purchase. Subsequent to that experience, online transactions will come easier.

Having both also means you need to consider online/offline synergies such as allowing purchases to be made online, with pick-up available where refunds and returns can be made either way. It's important to realize that from a customer's perspective there should be no difference in policy, refunds or service for a purchase made through the storefront or ecommerce site.

With online, there is never a dull moment, things are always changing and being a creative person I need this change to continue to feel alive and inspired. I thrive on change and being able to keep up is a nice challenge to have. I also like that I have the ability to engage with a lot more people via blog writing, social media, email, etc. than I ever could if I was only brick-and-mortar focused.

I consider myself lucky to have the experience of what it's like to own, operate and manage a storefront as well as being involved with various online businesses. I've learnt a lot! One of the most interesting lessons was the difference of how I needed to engage, entice and communicate with the customer in-store compared to online. What goes on in the customer's mind when browsing and deciding to purchase in store verses online is quite different and it's important to be aware of these major differences to ensure continued success.

Besides getting to know even more detail about the customer's journey in-store compared to online, I also became aware of the huge difference in costs and the complicated and stressful process involved in launching an actual physical shop compared to an online ecommerce store. I now realize I could have done a lot more planning when opening the boutique through testing concepts first prior to committing to an expensive lease.

Still trying to decide which model works best for your vision? Here's my own comparison list to help you make a smart decision:

Storefront

- Know your lease agreement inside out. What happens if you want to break the lease? What support will your landlord provide to attract customers? How often is a refit required?
- Make sure you are aware of all the sign-off requirements you need to have in place before opening and selling to the public.
- Ensure you allow extra time and budget for unforeseen issues such as delays in furniture arrival and required legalities.
- Make sure to have all of your insurances in place so you are covered the second someone steps into your shop.
- Road test all of your point of sale software and hardware; you would hate to have a successful launch only to discover sales were not able to be processed due to human error in installing or setting up the point of sale system.

Online

- Similar to a shop front, make sure to choose the perfect website platform which will allow you to easily make updates and changes to the front and back end of the site.
- Ensure the site is designed with SEO best practice in mind.
- Make sure to have a content strategy in place as you will need to hit the ground running with a lot of content to attract traffic.
- Road test your shopping cart, make sure there are not broken links or pages and that it is easy for the customer to place and order and pay for it.
- Ensure you have a great hosting company who cares about your success, provides a fast loading website and added security.
- Never trade without an SSL certificate, ensure you understand the basics of website security and have taken appropriate measures to keep your customer information safe.

Lastly, if being the boss of your own business is truly what you want, make sure you have enough savings to survive as you start or try to launch your idea. I was super fortunate to have the financial and emotional backing of my mother when I first ventured into business with the boutique. Without her constant mentoring and support, there would've been a lot of things I would have struggled (a lot more) with.

And don't be an over-planner! If you get too highly strung up with the small details, you will lose sight of the bigger picture. I prefer to do things keeping the 80/20 rule in mind. So whenever I tackle something, I think, "What can I do right now to increase or improve things by 80% without putting any more than 20% of my effort or time in?"

That same strategy can work for your dream business, too!

*****

DON'T BELIEVE THE HYPE ABOUT ONLINE BUSINESS

Magda de Berg, a successful online business entrepreneur, is the founder and owner of three innovative companies in Australia.

I started our online businesses based on a passion for learning new skills and a need to return to business whilst living in the country. After many years of working in and owning successful management consulting business our family decided it was time to leave the city for a quieter life in the country.

We purchased a farm on the coast in northern NSW, Australia and moved there to live with our kids surrounded by a slower pace, space and lots of fresh air. Six years later we still live at a slower pace surrounded by nature but now own three online businesses that provide that fast paced, competitive edge that I had started to miss.

How did I get here, well, online businesses are often born out of necessity. For me it was distance and a lack of commerce in our small town. For many online business owners there's a variety of reasons, being at home with the kids, needing additional income or simply not being able to find a product or service. The reason to start an online business is the easy part because it's an exciting decision with lots of blue sky. Growing your online business and making it the place to go on the internet is infinitely harder, fraught with some pitfalls but ultimately a hugely rewarding experience.

I don't profess to be an expert but I've learnt some things along the way which I'd love to share about working on or in an online business.

Passion. I discovered, to my great surprise, that after the dry corporate world I had inhabited for over two decades, children's toys and products delighted me in a way that consulting had never done. I did some research, looked at purchasing some toy businesses and ultimately decided to start online. It's been quite a few years now and I'm still that big kid at heart who opened her own online toy store! Passion for your business is key; it will come out in everything you do and how you communicate.

Isolation. In my office, I am a one-woman band. Sure our business has a warehouse and logistics staff, marketing staff and programmers but they all work remotely from my office here on our farm. Sound like a dream ? It certainly can be, I look out my office window and see our cattle walking past and enjoy the sun glittering off the dam, and after all everyone is just one phone call or email away. There are days, however, when things go wrong in the warehouse or Google punishes us for a programming error and I'd dearly love to just turn to a colleague and discuss. Meeting new people is also limited. In my old role as a consultant, I would meet at least two new people a day; now those meetings are over the phone more than face to face. In the end, I've got around the problem of being relatively isolated by making regular trips to visit our warehouse operations, suppliers and attend conferences where I can broaden my horizons again and feel refreshed to return.

Perseverance. Like in any area of life, you often read of online businesses that were an overnight success. Scratch a little deeper and you realize that overnight means 5 to 10 years of hard work without huge rewards. Bottom line: everything takes time. You can pop up a webpage in a couple of days but it will take 12 months for Google to take it seriously (and that's if you do everything right!) and even longer for customers to start talking or posting online about you to get you that word of mouth momentum that makes all the difference and gives you organic growth. Keep going. Seek help if you need it, but keep going.

Beware. Unless you are an online IT expert and have worked in other online businesses, beware of companies selling easy solutions for difficult problems. One of the most challenging areas of online business is Search Engine Optimisation, it takes time and effort but it's absolutely essential to the success of your online enterprise. I've learnt the hard way not to use SEO experts. After 12 months of work and over $15,000, our SEO experts had achieved three keywords on the first page of Google and a total of 300 questionably valuable back links. SEO should never be that expensive or that ineffective. It does take time and effort in ensuring your webpage contains unique content and delivers what your customer is seeking, so when you're looking for SEO assistance first read everything you can about SEO so you have the knowledge to ask your SEO expert the right questions. Looking back, I certainly wish I had done the research first.

Outsource. Any business - whether online or traditional brick and mortar - should consider outsourcing some part of their operations. In our case, we outsource our website coding to a company in India, whose skills and speed far outweigh suppliers in Australia. Outsourcing provides us access to skills which might not be readily available to us otherwise, and in the case of online business going global for certain skills makes both financial and business sense.

Enjoy. It's your business so enjoy it! If you find after the first few months that your online business is not enjoyable, you might need to reassess the business or your own mindset. There are times in any business which are stressful and cause you to tear your hair out. Unfortunately, these are often unavoidable, but if you truly enjoy your business you will meet these issues head on and work through them. I still wake up every day ready to jump into another day at the office, getting a note from a customer thanking us for the advice on a suitable toy or because we express-mailed that crucial plaything just in time for a birthday is reward enough for me for the times that things don't go to plan.

The truth of it is that a successful online business

still needs an investment in time and money, commitment, passion and a drive to solve problems quickly. The good news is that there are solutions to every business problem. If you have a passion for online business, then I say go for it! Just make sure you enter the sector with your eyes wide open, plenty of investment dollars and a willingness to see past the hype.

BALANCE AND BOUNDARIES

My husband nudged me out of a deep sleep to say that my office telephone was ringing. I groggily rolled over, opened one eye, and took note that the bedside alarm was reading 3 a.m.

There is rarely anything promising about a phone call that comes at that hour. If you're a parent, there's the dread that one of your offspring has just been in an accident or is in jail. If you're a business owner, the first thought is that there's been a break-in at your store or a fire at the factory. If you're the head of a country, it could mean anything from a terrorist attack to a giant asteroid plummeting toward Earth and anticipated to make impact in the next half hour.

Seeing as how I don't fit any of these situational conditions – and also pretty sure that the lottery commission wasn't calling to tell me I had this week's winning numbers – I was hard-pressed to fathom who in their right mind was trying to reach me before the sun was even up. My husband watched as I padded out the bedroom door and down the hall. Whether as a show of support (in case it was a legitimate crisis) or just curiosity, he and the dog soon joined me.

The caller – one of my ghostwriting clients – was already leaving a peppy message, the gist of which was that he was working on his blog, got stuck trying to find the perfect phrase, and figured I could just give him one off the top of my head. Now it's not as if this guy lives in – oh, say Holland, and that he didn't do the time-zone math while he was having his lunch. We live in exactly the same time zone, which made his call all the more inexcusable. What possible urgency existed that he couldn't have sent the same question via email to be opened when I was actually awake?

"So why didn't you pick up?" my husband asked, recognizing I was peeved enough to deliver a well deserved earful to the caller for disturbing my slumber.

"Because I'm not due at work for another six hours," I replied. And went back to bed.

When you're a sole proprietor – and especially if you conduct the majority of your business from a home office – establishing and reinforcing boundaries is one of the biggest challenges. It's not just about the need for a healthy balance between your personal and professional priorities; it's about training your clients to respect that you're not "on call" for them 24/7. In concert with this is a similar (mis)interpretation that "freelance" means you're free day and night, weekends, holidays and even when you're sick.

Granted, there's going to be an emergency now and then that requires you to don your super-hero cape and go rescue someone. Readers be warned, however: the first time you bend your own rules, make non-emergency exceptions, and start answering your home office phone during dinnertime or at 3 in the morning, you're giving your clients permission to devalue your time and services as well as your privacy.

Your business may not be brick-and-mortar but your mindset needs to embrace a steel resolve to keep it operating as professionally as possible.

*****

WHEREVER I LAY MY HAT

Michelle Tupy (currently based in Cusco, Peru) is a professional ghostwriter who quite happily spends most of her time behind the scenes writing blog posts, articles, e-books and Facebook commentary on behalf of busy entrepreneurs.

Hunting down cafes in the middle of the Sacred Valley, Peru to get a good Internet connection; sitting in crowded internet cafes in Changchun, China to respond to emails; and huddling in my van in the middle of a campground in Saskatchewan, Canada while uploading blog posts, is all part and parcel of my working life. And I wouldn't have it any other way. Not constrained by four walls or even one country, my office is wherever I call home at that particular moment in time.

Why? A good friend asked me this question and it made me think profoundly about why I do what I do. To me it is the norm. I met my husband in China over 10 years and 2 children ago and we have been travelling the world ever since. I like to experience what life has to offer and have never equated the word "home" with bricks and mortar or one singular location.

My laptop is my constant (as well as my husband and kids) and organisation is key to travelling and working around the world. I create with words - writing e-books, blog posts, social media updates and articles on anything and everything on behalf of others; a ghostwriter is seemingly the best term for what I do.

When physically relocating from town to town or even country to country, I ensure that all the larger tasks are tackled prior to the actual move, and I only do what is absolutely necessary to please the clients, make the deadlines and save my sanity.

A good Internet connection is a must and while at times it can be difficult to achieve, without it I would not be able to do what I do. Twenty years ago my lifestyle choice would have been impossible but today I am able to enjoy the freedom it gives and balance it with the needs of my clients.

As I essentially operate as a freelance writer, there are no requirements for work visas, permits or licenses for the various countries I choose to work in. And language is rarely a problem as most of my work is based online with clients who speak English either as a first or second language. I don't need to understand the intricacies of Mandarin or Spanish, which I am extremely grateful for! While the English language comes relatively easy to me, secondary languages do not, and I would struggle to write even the most basic of social media updates in a language other than English.

Good communication is essential to maintain with all my clients so they are aware that I am still approachable and contactable if necessary. I consistently advise them of my travel plans and always ensure them their work will still be done without issue. And I follow through. You are only as good as your reputation – and a missed deadline will undoubtedly reduce any future credibility you have to offer.

I choose to simplify my life and run all of my finances through my home country. Opening bank accounts in foreign countries can be full of difficulties that I just don't have time to micromanage. Paypal can be a traveller's best friend when managed correctly and ensures that your payments will not be interrupted. Travelling with zero income, I would imagine, would be very difficult to manage.

As a sole proprietor, I love the beauty of travelling and

working nationally and internationally. While I operate online the majority of the time for work purposes, I choose not to have a smartphone or a mobile phone when I am away from the home or "offline". It allows me to experience the life of living in diverse locations without getting bogged down with unnecessary interruptions. I fully comprehend I am seemingly at odds with my career choice and the technology it utilizes; however I find it hard to embrace the here and now with a smartphone beeping at every opportunity.

You don't need to be limited by your location, nor do you need to have an established business in your home country before you relocate. I started my online career in China – for better or worse – and have maintained it while living in Australia, Peru and Canada to date (not necessarily in that order).

Holidays can be taken as and when you decide and according to your schedule. No four weeks paid annual leave for me! I can hang out on a beach as long as I like (should I choose to do so), provided the online connection can satisfy my needs.

One of the biggest problems I face as a ghostwriter is how to best source my clients. This would be true, however, regardless of where my home base was. Most foreign countries have strong expat communities which you can tap into. In fact, I recently joined a writer's club in Cusco, Peru of all places. Online networking is important to any solo entrepreneur who works online; connect with others on LinkedIn, Facebook, Twitter and other online and offline communities and develop those contacts as best you can. The wider your circle of contacts, the more chance of someone needing or recommending your services. Word of mouth is a powerful tool.

You may also be able to link up with other writers or organisations that can pass work on to you for ease. In fact these days, most of my work comes from one particular source meaning I can focus more on the writing and less on the marketing.

While my situation may not suit everyone, it does allow others to see the potential in being able to work from home, wherever Home may be.

*****

FULL-TIME EVERYTHING

Sarah O'Bryan is a dream-chaser, mom, coffee-lover and author, whose book "Business and Baby at Home" explores the joys and challenges of working from home while balancing family life.

When you run a business from home, your work life and your personal life intertwine, boundaries are blurred and some days it's hard to distinguish between the two at all. As a business owner and mom to three children, aged one to eight years, I know the challenge all too well. The trick becomes making your environment work for you, rather that it being detrimental to what you're trying to achieve. We all know there are many benefits to running a home office, but what do you do when you feel like you're drowning under the pressure of the to-do list? What happens when you also have the added impact of being a parent? It comes down to balance and boundaries.

Balance is often something people are searching for in the first place. But sadly, balance is one of the first things to go once a home business is successfully up and running.

Work/life balance seems to be talked about everywhere at the moment. I read an interesting quote recently that said, "Work life balance is never achieved, it's only maintained." I tend to agree. It's that constant shifting of time and focus. I think it's hard to define - which is why it can be a bit elusive - because it looks different to different people. For some, it may be about achieving work goals while still going for a run every day. For others, it may be having time to play with your children after school. So to start, a good exercise is to write down what balance looks like for you.

Once this is established, here are some strategies to keep your balance in check:

- Keep a work-in-progress (WIP) list at all times so you have a record of your jobs. Update this throughout the day so nothing slips through the cracks. Go over it at the end of your workday to help you switch off and relax, knowing that everything is in place. This also means you start your day with a clear direction of what needs to be done first.
- Set reasonable lead times for yourself so that when

you're particularly busy you're not overly stressed trying to deliver on time. It's better to surprise a client by getting a job done early rather than it being late. If it's taking longer than you expected, retain clear communication with the customer, assuring them you're doing the best you can and that they're a top priority.

- Maintain a strong routine that enables you to get your work done. A lack of routine can result in shapeless and unproductive days with no progress. We all know as a parent, you can get to the end of a day and think where did the time go? So create and stick to a routine that works for you and allows blocks of time for working through your WIP.

- Know when and what to outsource. Maybe there are some responsibilities you can pay somebody else to do? Help comes in many forms; a gardener, a cleaner, an admin assistant, or the occasional babysitter. Think about the tasks that are zapping your time, or the jobs you don't particularly enjoy. This leaves you with more time to do what you are really great at.

- Have designated 'switch-off' times. Allow for 'on' and 'off' times throughout your day. For example, you may allocate 10-11a.m. to responding to emails, 12-2 p.m. to working on projects, then 3 p.m.-7.p.m. is dedicated family time. By having set rules, you'll also find you're more productive because the limited time creates a deadline for you. Procrastination goes out the window!

- Set short and long-term goals for both personal and professional achievements. These may be setting financial benchmarks, acquiring a number of new clients, or getting to Pilates once a week. It's a huge encouragement and as you tick them off they give direction to keep you on track for where you want to go.

Another factor that contributes to balance is boundaries. From physical boundaries, such as how your work space is set-up, to personal boundaries. What do you do when you're on deadline and your girlfriend wants to call-in for coffee?

It's really important to have a designated area that is your business space, and whilst this may look different for different people, the key word is 'respect'. You, as the business owner, need to respect it by making sure you have everything you need. No one has time to be searching for the power charger when there's a deadline to be met! Also, and probably more importantly, everyone else should respect it too, including your spouse and family.

It's totally okay to get protective of your zone! If you need an office environment, your own room is ideal, even better if it has a lock on the door. If you're easily distracted or like to listen to music while you work, a workspace away from the main living areas can help. Another important factor is whether you receive deliveries or if customers or clients need to visit. A lot of people convert their garage, as there's plenty of room, and it's quite separate. This often means you're not freaking out about having a clean house every time a client drops by.

Another effective strategy is setting up a separate phone line. Then you know whether it's a work call or personal call. Depending on which hat you're wearing, your business hat, or your "I'm making afternoon tea for my children" hat, you can respond accordingly. It's perfectly okay to let personal calls go to the answering machine if you're working and vice versa. It also helps communicate the message that you're busy, and not available 24/7, just because you're at home.

Really, the only person that can create balance, and set strong boundaries is you. Through self-control, you can choose to go for that run, or switch off your phone for the day. With today's technology it's very easy to be constantly checking your email; however, this can create a feeling of constant pressure and stress. So too, can not setting a clear definition between work and play, mentally and physically. Create a schedule, factor in work and non-work time zones, and stick to it. Check-in with the goals you set for yourself, it's a great way to make sure you're staying on-track.

*****

ME, MYSELF AND I (AND A DOG NAMED BARNEY)

John Churchman, creator/publisher of School Video News – an online TV and Film Production resource - brings decades of advertising, sales/marketing, and consulting expertise to whatever venue he visits.

As I hung up the phone I wanted to start dancing around at our little three bedroom, 900 square foot home in excitement. I had just been offered an exclusive seven Midwestern State Territory chock full of fortune 500 companies. My own territory with a hot new software product with no competition and an awesome commission plan! Truly a salesman's dream come true. All I had to do now was convert the leads that were sent to me and sit back and rake in the cash.

But here's the rub: I would be working from my house, I would have no secretary for correspondence or to set up travel plans, there was no marketing department to generate or qualify those leads, I would have to do my own contract negotiation and except for delivering product and sending out the invoice, I was totally on my own. Truly a new experience but one that I felt I could master.

It's a scenario that every sole proprietor can relate to. Specifically, "Whee! I'm my own boss" and "Eeek!" I'm my own boss!"

Feeling confident after doing this successfully for about a year and a half, I decided that I would take on a second project I could do in conjunction with the first. Now normally this would entail moving into larger office space, hire a secretary, buy more furniture, etc. In my case, however, it only required moving the crib into my office! You guessed it: Fatherhood. With a wife who worked out of the house, I found myself managing my territory for the aforementioned hot new software product *and* taking care of a newborn. Coffee breaks quickly became diaper breaks. The workday could and often did get hectic.

I remember one morning I was on the phone with a prospect that just couldn't wait to buy our product. Nicholas the child was soundly asleep in his crib, Barney the dog was soundly asleep under my desk when the FedEx man came trudging up the sidewalk, finger poised to hit the doorbell (which of course, he did). Barney the dog started barking to which my prospect asks, "You have a dog in your office?" "Oh," I replied, "didn't I tell you, I'm blind! That's my seeing eye dog Barney". At this point I could've gotten him to buy almost anything I wanted.

The silence on his end was deafening. By this time Nicholas the child had awakened and had started screaming so I thought it was probably a propitious time to admit that as a small startup company, we all worked out of our houses. It was an amazingly funny exchange, one I have repeated many times when asked about having an office in the home. By the way, he did end up buying our product.

That was almost thirty years ago. Since then, my at-home office/career and family/personal life have settled into a normal routine where the kids (now four of them but all grown up and gone) realize that when daddy goes off to the office, he is, for all intents and purposes NOT HOME! (Except for emergencies.) Working from home was probably one of the best opportunities ever presented to me. I don't think it would have been a successful experience right out of school or as a first job or two but, at the time, it opened up many doors professionally and mentally.

Being a very social creature, however, I need to talk about Social Interaction (or lack thereof) in the at-home environment. No more hanging around the water-cooler. No more watching the construction site out the office window. No more ambling down the corridor to cleanse your thoughts about the latest sticky project. It's all You! The phone and emails don't always cut it. I found that my social network became the waitresses where I would often escape to lunch or the grocery store personnel where I would frequently shop to get out of the office. Amazingly, this had the same effect: It distracted me from issues on which I was working. In fact, it was probably even better than discussing with co-workers who often tend to compound the issues being discussed!

Time Management can be the "kiss d'mort" of someone starting out at home. You think, "Ah ha! Now I can do what I want, when I want to do it. No more boss breathing down my neck!" Well, friends, that boss is now You (and your bank account) When I was selling, the motto quickly became: You Don't Sell, You Don't Eat! And that is a great motivator.

On the positive side, remember all those times when you're lying asleep in bed at 3 a.m. and BOOM you have that great idea? Now all I do is throw on a robe (Sometimes! Don't ask!), go back to the computer and pound out an idea. I would venture a guess that statistics would bear me out when I say working from home is much more productive than the confines of the "normal" workday.

The Kitchen as a decompression chamber or how *not* to kill your kids and wife. I firmly believe that everyone needs a cool-down or decompression period at the end of the workday. It's either a trip on a commuter train, or a drive from city to suburb, office to home. Regardless, it's a time when you can mentally wind up the day and re-focus for life with family. Loving to cook (with a wife who didn't!), I used that kitchen prep time as my decompression period. That hour between the end of daddy's workday and dinner on the table was the buffer zone that probably kept the family (and me) sane!

When you're a sole proprietor and your daily commute is only from one end of the house to the other, you need to create your own decompression activities in order to gracefully segue from your work life to your home life. For me, it was cooking. For you, it could be exercising, playing computer games, spending a slot of time on a favorite hobby. Even walking the dog. You do have a dog, don't you? Dogs are great companions for sole proprietors because they remind you that all work and no play makes you a mightily dull human.

FINANCIAL CHALLENGES

It's a fact of life that when you have the time, you don't always have the money, and when you have the money, you don't always have the time. During the first years of your sole proprietorship, you're not likely to have a whole lot of discretionary funds *or* leisure hours available to you. Even a business that's profitable isn't necessarily synonymous with a positive cash flow, especially if you're extending credit to your customers for their purchases or you're having to buy materials and equipment upfront for a major job such as interior decorating or landscaping design services.

It's also not uncommon to spend more time fantasizing about your unlimited earning capacity (that *is* why you pursued this, wasn't it?) than looking at how a highly saturated market, increased competition and a mercurial economy will impact your pricing and, psychologically, the value you put on yourself. Additionally, newbie business owners often dwell on all of the problems that have gone *wrong* with their start-up rather than celebrating the successes that have actually gone *right* and striving to repeat them with gusto.

To put this in the context of personal relationships, you could stay bitter for years about a messy divorce and beat yourself up incessantly for having had bad judgment in choosing a spouse OR you could reflect on how proud you are of your children, how much you're enjoying your new neighborhood, and how excited you are to be going back to college, writing your first novel, and having more time for friends you neglected during your marriage. Really now, which scenario sounds healthier and more productive? Your ability to manifest positive outcomes derives from simply not recognizing their existence – and potential - back when you were in the throes of despair.

While it's fine now and then to look in the rearview mirror and say, "I wish I hadn't made some of those mistakes," your focus as an entrepreneur needs to be fixed on the road ahead and how you can incorporate into your journey less of the past-lane laments and more of the upbeat elements that met your expectations or, in fact, turned out even better than you had hoped.

*****

Joel Peterson is CEO, Pintoresco Advisors and was previously a senior executive with AT&T, British Telecom, BellSouth and a VP with U.S. and international banks.

Q: What are some of the biggest financial planning mistakes that sole proprietors tend to make when/starting running a business and why are these so detrimental to long-term growth?

A: The single biggest financial planning mistake that people make in starting a business, especially as a sole proprietor, is simply not making a financial plan. Often, people "back into" a business for themselves, by themselves. Sometimes it is a hobby or side activity that starts to consume more and more of your time. Sometimes it's your regular profession, but you've been laid off and need to make it on your own.

Because so many sole proprietorships happen organically, rather than as a genuinely thought out, planned business option that is pursued among a range of options available, most people don't start their sole proprietorship with any sort of financial plan. But as soon as you find that you are truly in business by yourself, for yourself, you need a plan.

Ben Franklin is credited with stating that failing to plan is planning to fail, and this statement is most true of financial planning. Cash needs to be thought of as the blood that a business needs to sustain its life. The bigger the business, the more cash it will need, just like in animals: elephants require more blood to stay alive than mice. If cash is the blood, then cash flow is the pulse. How much blood needs to be pumped through an animal's body to meet its requirement to stay alive? Just as with animals, the bigger the business, the greater the cash flow requirements.

The financial plan portion of a comprehensive business plan is the mechanism through which a business owner models, predicts, and projects potential cash and cash flow needs and requirements. A sound financial plan will let you know how much cash from outside the business will be required to launch the business. Remember, there is almost no business that is fully self-funding – meaning it generates enough cash from its operations that it needs no cash from outside its operations - from the very beginning. Essentially all businesses need to start life with a blood transfusion: an infusion of startup cash. Your financial plan will let you know how much this is likely to be. As long as your financial plan is sound, prudent, realistic, and conservative.

The next biggest mistake that people make, other than not planning at all, is planning unrealistically and too optimistically. Almost all people greatly underestimate the actual startup cash that a business will need. This is caused by underestimation of costs, time, and other resources, and overestimation of revenues, sales effectiveness, demand, and product or service pricing.

Factors that can lead to errors of *underestimation* include:

- Failing to account for ALL expenses (such as license fees, workers' comp, maintenance, repairs, replacements, rents, leases, renewal fees, legal services, advertising, and insurance, among many others);
- Underestimating the amounts of each expense (such as assuming your car or delivery vehicle won't ever break down or need repair)
- Underestimating the length of your sales cycle (most people assume they can make a sale with too little investment of time, energy, resources, and cash; a sale always takes longer than anticipated)
- Underestimating your inventory and supplies requirements
- Underestimating today's technology, IT, and communications needs and costs (many people forget to account for software licenses and ongoing help desk and other support services)
- Underestimating returns, refunds, or discounts demanded by customers or clients
- Underestimating logistical time frames and lead times required (such as the time it takes to print presentation material by a printer, including all the proofing to correct for all the errors)

- Underestimating the competition, both in numbers of and in their actions to undermine and defeat you.

Factors that often lead to errors of *overestimation* include:

- Overestimating demand for your product or services (such as assuming customer or order growth will happen sooner and grow at a faster rate than what will actually happen)
- Overestimating the pricing that you will be able to charge for services and products. As a small business, especially a sole proprietor, you will be a price taker, not a price setter. You will need to take the prevailing price in the market for your services or product, and likely below market. Because you don't have a national brand, great depth of bench (you're a sole proprietor), people will see you as less reliable, riskier, and more vulnerable, and therefore they will be less willing to pay you the prevailing price. Don't kid yourself that you can exact a premium because you're unique or of better quality. Especially at the beginning of a business, you will need to "buy" customers away from their current provider of the service or product. This means deep discounts, free samples, or both.
- Overestimating the value of relationships and friendships. This is business, not a Bible study or Talmud readings club. Your friends and past professional relationships will not go out of their way, take risks, expend relationship or political capital for you or your business – unless there is clear benefit in it for them. As the saying goes in Hollywood: it's show business, not show friends.
- Overestimating the uniqueness, quality, or special appeal of your service or product. Most sole proprietors go into business because they are passionate about what they do; the services offer or products that make. Others may not share in your passion and may not see your baby the way you do.
- Overestimating the attention and impact of advertising and marketing. To you, your ad may be

amazing, catchy, obvious, and memorable. To nearly everyone else, they're too busy with their world to have noticed it or remember it.

- Overestimating customer loyalty. Remember, they are your customers, not your friends. From their view, they are paying you and therefore doing you a favor. If they find a cheaper or better option, their "loyalty" may vanish.

- Overestimating your own energy, abilities, charm, and drive. Despite your best intentions, you will experience illnesses, bad days, people who just don't like you, family problems, marital challenges, children's school demands, and family deaths and tragedies. You will not be able to work as hard, as long, or as effectively as you may want to assume.

In summary: the biggest financial planning mistake that many businesses, especially sole proprietorships, make is failing to have a financial plan. The next biggest mistake is to have a plan that is unrealistic. The vast majority of financial plans grossly underestimate the upfront and ongoing cash needs of the business and grossly overestimate the amount and timing of revenues – cash that the business will actually generate. Unrealistic financial plans usually are caused by not accounting for ALL costs, underestimating the costs that are accounted for, and overestimating the pricing, sales volumes, and demand for your services or products.

Q: Getting a loan when you're an "office of one" is a challenge but especially if what you offer clients is a service (i.e., consulting, writing, etc.) vs. a product. Accordingly, what can a sole proprietor do to get start-up funding and/or to prove s/he is a good risk for a business loan?

A: In general, using loans as startup funding is a bad idea. Taking on interest payments immediately even before the business has started generating any revenues puts enormous pressure on the business. If at all possible, you should start your business with equity funding, meaning that the cash used to startup the business buys ownership in the business, but does not create a debt or interest payment obligation.

If you do use debt to fund a startup, the only lending program that may make sense is a loan from the Small Business Administration (SBA). SBA loans are not given directly by the SBA but by independent commercial lenders and banks who underwrite (evaluate) the loan and your business' ability to service and pay back the loan. The SBA stands behind the bank and guarantees the loan's repayment in the event of default, if the bank followed all the SBA's guidelines and procedures.

Your startup business, especially if you are a service provider, will have few or inadequate hard assets (buildings, equipment, vehicles, patents, licenses, cash, land). Therefore, your business will not be able to provide or offer collateral. Lenders require a borrower to show that they either have proven cash generation history in their business, which a startup will not be able to show, or that it has enough liquidation value (how much are assets worth when having to do a forced sale) to cover the loan amount. Again something that a startup will likely not be able to show.

Therefore, SBA loans require your personal guarantee as well as the pledge of your assets, usually your home. Since more than 90 percent of new businesses fail, borrowing startup funds and pledging your home as collateral constitutes a greater than 90 percent chance that you will have to repay the loan from the value of your home. If you do not have enough equity in your home, then you are taking a greater than 90 percent chance of losing your home.

If you have good equity in your house, and you have a stable source of household income to cover the existing and a second mortgage (such as a spouse's income or primary job), then it may make sense to borrow a second mortgage to fund your startup. The caution is that this option should only be pursued if there is enough stable, dependable household income – outside of the startup business – to service the increased mortgage debt. If not, you are risking losing your house.

It's a different story if your business has been up and running for some time. Generally, banks and lenders want a minimum of 3 years of profitable operations, ideally 5 or more years. There are many lending programs that allow you to pledge future assets, such as receivables, or tangible assets, such as equipment. Typically, banks will lend up to 10 percent of the last year's revenues, as long as the last 2 years have been profitable and the revenues have been stable or growing. It becomes more difficult, if revenues and/or profits have noticeably declined.

Alternative ways to improve the ability to gain loans is to have someone else co-sign on your loan, if that person has better income, credit score, or more assets than you. However, most people are reluctant to join you in your indebtedness and risk having to repay the loan on your behalf.

Alternatively, you can explore private loans. You may have family or friends who would be willing to make a loan to you and may not use the same standards of underwriting or the same loan terms and conditions that commercial lenders do. The caution is that, if the loan terms are too lax compared to commercial loans, the IRS may deem it to be an equity investment and not a loan at all. This could cause penalties to the business and the lender with regard to how interest expense or income was reported on tax filings.

In summary, it is very difficult to find lenders and funds from loans for a startup company, especially a sole proprietorship. This is for a good reason. It is generally a very bad idea to fund the majority or all of the startup cash needs of a business with loans.

Q: **Why maxing out on credit cards to start a business is or isn't a smart move?**

A: Credit cards have one very good characteristic that makes potentially using them to help fund the startup of your sole proprietorship not completely a bad idea. But credit cards also have one very bad characteristic that may make using them as a source of startup capital a very bad idea.

Credit cards are unsecured credit lines. What this means is that the credit card company has no ability to take any of your (or if it's a business credit card, the business') assets. They cannot impound your car or house or bank account. What you have signed with a credit card company is a contract saying that you promise to repay all borrowings, fees, and interest (and usually any costs of collection).

This means that if you do not pay, then the only thing the credit card company can do is sue for breach of contract. They would need to win a court judgment against you, be awarded damages by the court, and then under a court order could place liens on assets or wages. This is a costly and lengthy process and most credit card companies will give a combination of loan forgiveness and loan payment restructuring (giving more time, reducing monthly payment, waving fees, etc.). Also, if you file for bankruptcy, they may not collect anything from you, depending on the amount of other debts and liabilities you have.

The very bad characteristic of credit cards is that they are some of the most expensive debt available. Their interest rates are very high, relative to other sources of loans and they add significant fees and penalties that add grossly to the costs of the credit card loan.

In general, borrowing money to start a business is a bad idea. The cash used to start a business should be mostly equity contributions. Using borrowings from credit cards may be a reasonable option if you have a timing issue, for example, if you know the business will be paid a large payment in a week that would more than cover the expenses that are due this week, then it may make sense to pay this week's expense with credit cards, and use the payment received next week to pay off the credit card balance.

The key point is to remember to immediately pay off the credit card when the revenue to do so arrives. The other key point is, you need to be very certain that the revenue payment will arrive when you expect it, otherwise, you will have potentially turned a bad situation into a worse one.

In summary: it is generally a very bad idea to max out credit cards as the primary or even partial way to fund the startup of your business.

Q: Keeping personal and business finances separate is a no-brainer. But what happens when your company starts to teeter financially (or worse, go under)? How do you ensure that it doesn't affect your personal credit?

A: The key to keeping your personal credit from being affected by the financial problems or failure of your business is to never make personal guarantees of business obligations. When your business is just starting, this may be difficult, because there may be no revenues, history, or few assets within the business.

Comingling personal and business finances may not necessarily cause any effect on your personal credit, but it is bad business and may lead to violations of tax rules, such as taking business deductions for personal expenses. Risking IRS and state tax board penalties and action is not a prudent path to take.

Additionally, mixing personal and business finances, such as using corporate lines of credit to purchase personal items or taking "loans" from the business for your personal use, may "pierce the corporate veil." What this means is that the courts and the IRS may decide that the corporation and you are not two different legal persons, but are actually the same legal person. In this case, any and all liabilities of the business become your personal liabilities.

Under the law, a business, even a sole proprietorship, if it is incorporated, is a separate legal person (living, breathing people are "natural" persons and incorporated entities, like companies and trusts, are "artificial" persons). But under the law, a person – natural or not – has the same rights and obligations under the law. Therefore, a company's obligations are the company's alone, unless you personally co-signed as a guarantor.

If there are no personal guarantees or other joint obligations if the company fails, its debts and obligations, financial and legal, stay with it and this does not affect your personal credit or legal obligation – in theory. In practice, lenders often require you to disclose if you have had a business bankruptcy even if you personally have not, and this information may affect lending decisions and risk analysis.

Also, if your company is sued, typically the suing party will also sue you personally as the owner or officer, claiming that you personally were responsible through your action or inaction or negligence. Usually the suit against the owner will not be successful if there has been a strong, consistent financial and operational separation between you, the natural person, and your business, the artificial person.

Because there may be much closer ties between the business and the owner in a sole proprietorship, it is all the more important that a sole proprietor go the extra mile to keep all personal finances and accounts separate and clear.

Having business insurance that protects you as the owner and manager in case of lawsuits will be helpful and is a prudent investment – and cost that needs to be included in your financial planning of the business.

In summary: always keep separate bank accounts, loans, and legal obligations (such as contracts – don't use your personally contracted electrician to do work for the business; have a separate contract between the business and the electrician). And avoid making any personal guarantees for your business obligations. If you follow these rules strictly, you can avoid negatively affecting your personal credit, even if your business fails.

THE ACCOUNTANT: A SOLE PROPRIETOR'S BEST FRIEND

In 1999, Steve Martin starred in *Bowfinger*, a comedy about an aspiring filmmaker so determined to make his first movie that he has spent his whole life accruing what he believes to be the magic amount that will make this quest a reality: $2,184. Convinced that this princely sum - and a luckless coterie of flunkies as desperate for fame as he is – will put him among Hollywood's elite, he embarks on a wild and crazy plan to make his *Chubby Rain* SciFi flick on the cheap by secretly filming a paranoid action star. What could possibly go wrong? Well, plenty…and especially considering that the script was penned by someone who should have had a tighter grip on the production's purse strings: Bowfinger's own accountant.

While the childlike naiveté to keep one's savings in a shoebox under the bed and the adult guile to engage in guerilla movie shoots is the stuff of hilarity in film, it's no laughing matter when you enter into your first business venture without the priceless guidance of a trained accounting professional. When you're taking the time to invest in a dream, it's paramount to make sure that when the tax man cometh, he doesn't taketh away all that you've worked for.

*****

Steven S. Tyre has been a CPA in the Los Angeles area since 1974 and formerly worked for international accounting firm of Coopers & Lybrand before starting his own practice specializing in taxes, estates, trusts and small businesses.

Q: When someone comes to you and says that they're going to go into business for themselves, what's the first advice you give them?
A: The first thing I ask them is "Tell me if you're ready." Have you researched someone else who's already successful in this business to make sure this is something you want to do, that you're competent to do, and that you

feel you can be successful at? Just *wanting* something isn't enough; you not only have to know what it is you're really getting into but also whether there's an actual consumer interest and need for it that's not already being met by a dozen similar shops around town.

I also tell aspiring business owners that they had better have a bankroll. Don't go into business short of money because 99 percent of the people who go the sole proprietor route are initially going to *lose* money. So how much is enough? Well, that's why you need to make sure you're aware of what all the costs of your chosen business are going to be. For example, if you think you're going to open a bakery, you better go out and see what all of the equipment's going to cost – the ovens, the mixers, the ingredient bins, the proofers, the display cases. It's not cheap! It's also not cheap to order your administrative supplies and then have to figure out where to store them. (Our own business uses an online vendor called Quill.com which allows us to do small-batch orders on supplies as they're needed.)

The next major thing to think about is what kind of government regulations are involved to run your business. If you're going to be doing it in your home, is your property zoned for commercial ventures? Have you researched whether your profession requires any special permits, certificates or licenses? If you're going to open a restaurant, you have to see what the health department's going to do, see what city licenses are needed, see if there are going to be any kind of entanglements that will kill your business before it even gets off the ground.

Are you planning to take credit and debit cards for the goods and services you offer? If you are, don't go through a bank for this. This is the common mistake most people make when they're in business for themselves because they think it's the most convenient. The truth is that it can also be more expensive. Establish a merchant account through a credit card processing firm instead. There's quite a difference in the processing charges and it's important to shop around and find the best rate.

Most importantly, make sure that in advance of going into business you've consulted an accountant to track your expenses and so that you can take advantage of all the tax laws that are involved in starting, running and growing a business.

Q: Is it more prudent to lease a space or buy one?

A: If you're not planning a home-based business and you're going to go out and get a different physical address, be very careful to check out the look and general upkeep of the neighborhood and ensure that the cost of remodeling a particular building to fit your business isn't going to put you *out* of business. It's extremely expensive to remodel these days and can also be time-consuming. This can delay your grand opening or cause you to have to close shop during renovations. Keep in mind, too, that if you're going to have a physical presence, the outside needs to be well maintained and you have to have signage so customers can easily find you. And if you offer other services, make sure that your clients know about them.

Most people don't have the money to buy a building but it's important to keep in mind that if you launch a successful business, the number one thing you want to do is buy the premises. The reason is that the rent will always go up; once you buy the building, you'll have a fixed cost. A business that's doing well and thriving in a good location is also going to attract people who will want to put their business near you. Let me give you an example. Our office is located in a heavily populated Chinese neighborhood. When my building came up for sale many years ago, I wasn't sure if I wanted to buy it. I talked to a friend of mine who was a big landlord and he told me that if I didn't buy it, the neighbors would and I'd be kicked out in a heartbeat. If your business is successful and your landlord is willing to sell – even if you have to pay more in order to purchase that building – not only will that purchase give you a fixed cost but it will also appreciate in value and someday when you close your business, you'll have something to sell and retire on.

Q: Even though a person considers himself or herself a "sole proprietor" that doesn't necessarily mean that they are just working out of their home as an individual. When deciding upon what business form to conduct your business as an individual (sole proprietor,

corporation, LLC, PC) what should someone be thinking about?

A: I like a sole proprietorship as a business model for an initial proprietor - which basically is a Schedule C – because it's the cheapest to run and the losses will be able to be written off against other income on their tax return. The second form I like which can be pursued after you become more successful is a Subchapter S Corporation. A Subchapter S is a corporation and what it allows you in certain circumstances is to save you money on Social Security taxes for yourself.

To keep things simple, a sole proprietorship is the right form until you make your first $50,000 in profit. When you've become that successful, then you should go to a professional and discuss whether to form an LLC, a Subchapter S or a C Corp. That's the magic number; once your business makes $50,000 profit, there are some tax situations that change and it makes the additional cost of an entity worthwhile.

Q: Insurance seems to be something that everyone has to be concerned about – what is the best way to make sure your business as a sole proprietor is protected against liability?

A: First of all, if you're in any kind of a trade group such as a lawyer, a doctor, a cement mason, etc., my recommendation is to go to your trade association and see if they have a liability policy available. A lot of times if you go directly to your trade association, they can get you a better deal than a general insurance agent. You could also go to someone who specializes in business insurance policies. It's very important to compare. Don't take the first deal you're offered. Prices vary greatly.

Also, make sure the amount of liability insurance you're buying is not too much and not too little. What's the worst case scenario that could happen to you? Once you know that, you can then get the proper coverage. If you're a professional, you also want to get malpractice insurance. If you're going to be renting, you want to get a tenant's insurance policy. Realize that your landlord's policy doesn't cover inside the walls in most cases. So if you're a baker, for instance, you have to get insurance to cover your oven, your storage and display cases, and your cash register.

And speaking of protecting stuff, it's critical that you always keep an off-premises back-up of your most important data. Your computer should be backed up in a zip drive or a disk that's taken off the premises on a daily basis. Or, for that matter, back it up to the Cloud. If the place burns down or you're burglarized, you want everything backed up in a place that's safe.

Q: Employees have a 401k or other retirement plans. As a sole proprietor, what should someone be thinking about in terms of retirement security?

A: Don't even worry about this until you're making $100,000. The reason is that most small business people will need every dollar they can get their hands on and the last thing they're going to do is have cash to fund a retirement plan. But when they do fund one, they really need to be aware of the fact that – if they have any employees – they'll have to fund it for all of their employees as well.

If you do an IRA, you're exempt from having to do that. If and when you find you have some extra money laying around, you can think about funding a pension plan. This can be a one-man 401k which is the one you can put the most into. It can also be a self-employed pension plan, an IRA, a ROTH IRA, or a ROTH 401k. You really have a lot of choices on that. I hate to plug a particular company but if a small business owner is looking to fund a pension plan but is dazed and confused and wants great information for free, go to Fidelity Investments. I have it on good authority they have a bunch of little nerds who sit in a back room somewhere that's called Retirement Services and they'll answer questions from here until the cows come home. If you decide to go with them, they'll also set up the right plan for you and are reasonably priced. They usually don't charge administration costs because they make it on the sale of mutual funds. Another one worth checking out in Vanguard Investments. I highly recommend both of them.

Q: The Affordable Care Act has drastically changed the health insurance environment. What should a sole proprietor be thinking about in terms of having health insurance?

A: Everything is changing so rapidly when it comes to health insurance that in order for this book to be the most helpful to readers, my advice is to check out whatever the current situation is. I will have to say, though, that you need to look at the exchanges and if you have no other income and your business is losing money, you can probably get health insurance for almost free. You want to look at what your state – or if you're overseas, your country – offers based on your income. This is clearly an evolving situation since Obamacare came into play. The best way to check is to find an insurance agent in your locale who can advise you. The rules differ so much from state to state and country to country that there's really no one-size-fits-all-situations.

Q: As a sole proprietor with no employees, there is no need to worry about workers' compensation insurance. That's correct, isn't it?

A: Yes, that's correct. In some states, however, it's worth just to protect yourself to sign up for state disability insurance. Readers might want to set up a payroll for themselves so they can participate in state disability insurance.

Q: How about a situation where a sole proprietor is putting on an event and needs some volunteers or student interns. They're not paying them but what happens in the context of an unpaid helper having an accident?

A: They need to consult their liability carrier.

Q: What unique estate planning issues are created by being a sole proprietor?

Absolutely none...unless the business is worth a lot of money. If your business is approaching a value of $5 million, then you should consult an estate tax attorney. And just as an aside, if you happen to have a lot of shirttail relatives interested in your will, never leave them a percentage of the estate; leave them a specific dollar amount instead. If, say, they each get $10,000 instead of "x" percent, they'll have no legal right to the rest of the estate because they have only been given a set amount of money.

Q: My product suddenly is in great demand. I don't want to take on a partner, but I would like an

extra set of hands to fulfill orders. What's the best way to accomplish this?

A: Depending on the complexity of the business, the best way to do it is look at competitors and see if there's someone there who might want to help. If it's a temporary need for a specialized business, find someone who's perhaps retired but knows the craft and can do the job. That happens a lot in the legal field. For instance, a lawyer will need an additional lawyer and, in asking around, finds that there's someone who used to work at a different firm but is now a stay-at-home mom. You can call her up and say, "Hey, Susie, I have some files that need to be reviewed. Is this something you could while your child's at school or taking a nap?" It's a good way for them to make extra money and for you to get extra help when you're in a crunch.

What I actually tell people, though, is that when it's time to hire their first employee – and I've done this all my life – the best possible person to get is a mother. Seriously. If you let the mother do what she has to do with her children – meaning when they get sick or she needs to do something at their school – a mother will be the best employee you can ever get. They don't leave, they're loyal, they're honest, they're great. I love hiring mothers with children that need or want to go back to work. It's also important to create flexible hours for them. On top of that, I've found that mothers in general don't need any supervision. They know the hours they're supposed to be here, they know the work that needs to get done and they already have experience at multi-tasking taking care of their families.

Another tip: It's important that you don't hire someone who has had a bunch of different jobs and has a history of not staying at any of them for very long. You also want to check a prospective candidate's criminal record and talk to their last employer.

I really like college students, too. They're young, they have a lot of energy, they're smart and if your business is technologically based, they're the ones who are going to be able to understand it because they were born doing it.

Q: I am starting to get calls from investors and people who want to be partners and "expand" the

business. **What should I be concerned about if I want to bring others – whether as an investor or someone who will participate in the running of the business?**

A: Well, for one thing you should be concerned about losing control of your own business. How much do you know about the investor? What's his expertise in the business? What's he going to bring to the business? Personally, I'd prefer to get a bank loan than a partner. I hate partners. There's an advantage that it splits the work. On the other hand, I hate that feeling of wondering whether I'm doing my fair share or whether they're doing their fair share and the relationship could get ugly.

Q: I want to make sure I am running my business legally – what kind of checklist should I have to make sure I have all the permits, licenses, or authorizations I need to have to do business?

A: The first place to check is the city you're located in. Check with a competitor. Join the chamber of commerce. Find an attorney that handles that kind of business. Research your kind of potential business on the Internet. For instance, Google "problems with being a plumber".

The most important thing about being an entrepreneur is that when things go wrong is to be very pro-active. You're never going to get a lawsuit if you try and remedy the situation. For example, if I ever have a situation in which a client is penalized on a tax filing or interest on a tax filing that was my fault, I always pay it. Lawsuits come about when a client comes to you with a complaint and you don't get back to them.

Always answer your clients' calls within 24 hours. Put that on your business answering machine, by the way. "This is Joe. Leave a message. I'll get back to you within 24 hours." It has to be *your* voice, too, and not one of those generic recordings. If I call someone and I get a generic recording, how do I know I've even reached the right number? I've also noticed a lot of entrepreneurs run their business off their cell phone. Do not leave the generic AT&T lady outgoing message on it. Use your own voice for the recording, even if it's just the phone number.

Q: Any other advice you'd like to add for today's sole proprietors?

A: There are tax advantages in hiring your young children. If they're under 18, you can pay them a salary and in most cases there are no payroll taxes.

If you have a normal family, have a picture on your wall so that anyone who comes in knows that you're a steadfast individual. You want to nonverbally create credibility with your clients and customers and pictures are a great way to do that. This assures them that you're stable and you're not going to run away when they need service.

And as a final note, when shopping for an accountant, you want someone who has at least 20 years of experience as a sole practitioner. You especially don't want someone who has just left a big firm to go out on their own. The price of an accountant is not as important as the years of experience because he's going to save you more money on your taxes than he's going to charge you.

FINE TUNED BUDGETS
AND FINE PRINT LEGALITIES

Ignorance can be bliss but what you don't know about business finances, insurance, licenses, certifications, contracts and confidentiality agreements can put your sole proprietorship at risk in a heartbeat. Consider, for instance, the following real-life tales from the trenches:

Evelyn (Esthetician)
Ontario, CA

I worked for 9 years at a beauty salon in a major department store doing facials. I had dozens of clients who liked me and said they'd follow me anywhere. Since I wanted my own place, my husband converted our garage. It also had its own separate entrance. When I gave notice at the salon, I thought I'd have two weeks to copy all my clients' names and numbers. My manager made me leave on the very spot that day and I couldn't take anything with me. I hadn't really read the contract I signed 9 years before but there was some clause in it that said I couldn't steal any clients of the salon if I ever left. I don't think of it as stealing if they all liked me and knew that I might leave someday anyway. Other people have told me this is a standard thing but I had never heard of it. And so I was without a job and income and without enough clients to make my own salon the success it should have been.

Ron (Computer Geek)
Aurora, CO

My best buddy and me were always asked by family and friends to fix their computers for them because we were good at it. Mostly we just did it for free and for fun but then we decided we could make money going into business together. He had a girlfriend and two kids and I lived by myself so we decided that between my kitchen table as a work space and a van for making repair calls, we didn't need to rent a store, which we also couldn't afford as a start-up! After about four months of doing pretty good, he suddenly got a job at a computer store and I was on my own. It wouldn't have been so bad being my own boss except he felt he should get half the profits since he fronted half the launch money for "our" idea. We never put anything in writing about this because we were best friends and didn't think we had to. Notice I said "were best friends." He took me to the small claims court and we're no longer talking.

Nita (Grant Writing)
Fort Worth, TX

After four years of doing grants development for nonprofits, I started my own agency and even got my own small office downtown because it made me look official. Work slowly started coming in and then I suddenly landed a huge project. Their files needed lots of photocopying and since I was going to be on the phone all day, I asked my sister's daughter if she'd come in that day to help me. Part way through she said she was going to run out and get a soda. I said okay since I'd hear from the next room if anyone came in the door. Well, someone did while I was on the phone and it was the person I had that big project with. When he saw my niece left all their confidential papers right out in plain sight on the counter for anyone to see, I lost that job right on the spot. My niece didn't use good judgment or common sense but I now know it was my fault not to explain to her those files contained privileged info.

Sharell (Word Processing)
Baltimore, MD

I used to type for people at night and on weekends to bring in extra money. Because I am fast and accurate, it was hard to keep up with demand and someone I knew at work said I should just make it a fulltime business and work from home. I liked that idea, especially because I wouldn't have to take a train or a bus across town anymore and go to an office when the weather was too rainy, too snowy, too hot, etc. At the end of every day, I would run backup files of everything I typed for my clients (I did some bookkeeping for some of them, too) and I kept the backup files in a separate place. When you're a one-person business, you never think anyone would try to steal your stuff and so it never occurred to me I should have separate business insurance in case anything happened. Which it did. Big Time. I wish I had talked to someone about what I needed to do to protect my investment in Me. What's worse is that some of my clients' information was super confidential and because I wasn't prepared for what happened, that information was all compromised and these people will never hire me again.

Billy (Food Truck Operator)
Miami, FL

I ran my own food truck.....for five weeks!!! I thought I did *everything right when I bought an existing tricked-out food van, got a city business license, and got a passing grade from the local health and sanitation inspectors. Plus everybody said the food I sold was awesome and not like anything else they ever had. Since there are millions of food trucks all over the city, I assumed you just parked wherever you could find the most people (like office buildings just before lunch hour) and a parking space and it would be easy street. No one ever told me there are parking and vending restrictions and that the restaurants don't hesitate to call the police and report you if they think you're stealing business from them. Trying to be your own boss and just sell good food isn't as easy or fun as everybody thinks it is.*

J.T. (Ghostwriting)
Pittsburg, PA

If you have never written a business contract before, you'll probably make lots of costly mistakes, mistakes that sometimes cost you much more than if you had just hired a lawyer in the first place. I ghostwrite novels and memoirs for clients and with each one I learn more details I should have spelled out in the initial contract. These include due dates, payment schedules, and (especially) how many rewrites a client can reasonably request. I take pride in my work and I want them to be happy but some of them are just impossible to satisfy. As an example, I was at the halfway point on a romance novel for one client when she decided she was tired of the plot and wanted me to start all over with a completely different premise and characters! In another case, a client died while I was awaiting the second half payment of the completed manuscript. The spouse maintained that since she wasn't going to have her husband's book published now that he was dead, there wasn't any reason to pay me for the second half of it. And those are just two of the nicer stories I could tell about clients from Hell.

Ken (Costume Rentals)
Glendale, CA

Although I knew I couldn't compete with the major studios that have huge wardrobe departments, there's lots of indie filmmaking going on and I decided to start a costume rental biz by myself. My brother had a large, well-insulated storage space I could use and so the biggest start-up expense was purchasing costumes and doing outsourcing to have new ones made. I guess I made the common entrepreneurial mistake of thinking that because my credit was good, I could max out on a few cards and just pay them off as business started rolling in. The problem was that my launch came just two weeks before a major strike that lasted forever. My actor friends (in a show of solidarity) put a halt to their own production plans so they could go stand in picket lines. Rather than step back and assess the situation, I continued to spend and then, to try and cut corners, engaged the services of some people who weren't really aboveboard. Consulting with an attorney, a business planner, and a CPA might have saved me from the ruin that followed and the heartache of having to fold before I ever got the chance to spread my wings.

Bev (Lunch Delivery)
Boston, MA

My boyfriend liked the sandwiches I always made for his lunch and the guys who worked with him said my sandwiches were something they'd buy. So he decided to write down orders after work and I'd get up real early and make a basket of sandwiches for him to sell in the break-room the next day. Someone complained and he got written up for doing personal business on state property. So a friend who lived near his office said I could put out a sign and sell my sandwiches in her driveway from a cooler in the back of my car. I didn't just get in trouble with the police but the city and the public health department, too.

It also goes without saying that no matter how informal/friendly the relationship (i.e., family, friends) or simplistic the task in which your sole proprietorship is engaged, getting the basics in writing will save you a boatload of grief if disagreements ever arise, payments have to be chased down, or the relationship ever needs to be dissolved.

*****

GET YOUR FINANCES IN ORDER!

Deirdre Morhet, founder of BASC Expertise, has developed a sharp eye for how businesses get bloated with inefficiencies, specifically when it comes to cash flow and taxes, and how they can retool for a sleeker, smoother, strategically focused organization.

A sole proprietorship is the simplest form of business; however, it is important to understand how everything is linked to the individual personally. Financial education, stability, and credit worthiness are very important for the very reason that, as a sole proprietor, the business and person are one in the same. The business itself is not taxed separately; the sole proprietorship income is your income. Keeping track of personal finances as well as business and keeping them separate is extremely important.

If sole proprietors do not address their personal financial situation it will undoubtedly bleed over into their business. Good personal financial habits breed good business financial habits. Bad financial habits can ultimately be the demise of a business startup.

It's a good idea for sole proprietors to save for an emergency and retirement fund; specifically:

- Establish a budget and ensure that you budget a dollar amount that will go directly to an emergency account before anything else (making it automatic is ideal either via direct deposit or an automatic transfer). A good number to shoot for is between 3-6 months-worth of living expenses. As a business owner with dynamic cash flow issues, this can be more difficult. Continually look through financials to identify inefficiencies that can be cured and redirect that saved money to the emergency fund.

- We always recommend having the emergency savings fully funded before anything else. After that, the retirement savings plan can be implemented in much the same way. Setting up an IRA and having direct transfers into that account every month is a great way to put a retirement savings plan on autopilot to ensure that it is being funded. Once an investment plan is implemented, the account can be setup to make automatic periodic purchases of mutual funds or other investments at designated intervals (weekly, monthly, quarterly, etc.).

Investments

Sole proprietors may consider investing in stocks within a well-balanced portfolio. For one, you have more control over harvesting gains or losses for tax purposes in order to help offset potential gains or losses in a given year. On dividend paying stocks, the tax you pay on qualified dividends is less than you would pay on interest you may be receiving on bonds, savings account or CDs. Also, the growth rate of stocks over a long period of time has generally proven to be one of the best ways to build wealth.

It is always advisable to work with a trusted financial advisor with specific expertise in the stock and mutual fund markets. Unless one has a background in stock trading, attempting to buy individual stocks and "play the market" is really a great way to gamble away ones investment funds.

Debt

Debt can be a killer for a business owner. If you start a business with a large amount of debt, you need to immediately be bringing in more revenue than someone who starts with their debts paid down or paid off. It is certainly more advantageous to start a business when a sole proprietor has limited personal debt outside of a mortgage or car payment. That being said, I don't think that having debt, in and of itself, should be the sole reason someone decides whether or not to go into business. If they have a well thought out business plan or a built-in client-base to step into, it may still be viable.

Home Equity

There are advantages and disadvantages to using home equity to find the expansion of the home. The potential downside is that you're attaching a non-business asset as collateral for your business and we generally advocate for more separation. If the business goes under, the house goes with it. The benefit is that their primary residence may be the business owner's largest asset and only viable way to get the funding needed to build out the space. In my opinion, what it would boil down to is the history of the business and whether, financially, they're trending up or down. If they are trending down, I would advise against it.

Finance/Money Mistakes to Avoid

Sole proprietors want to avoid making the following top five finance/money mistakes:

1.   Carrying too much credit card debt

2. Cosigning loans for others: What seems like a nice gesture to help others can often put you in a bind especially if there are ever issues with the loan and you become financially obligated.
3. Using your home as a piggy bank: Be careful using all your home equity even if it's for business expenses
4. Raiding retirement funds: Using money saved for retirement early often creates issues if it not for an unavoidable emergency. Getting back to where you were at is often not treated as a priority setting you back years.
5. Excessive Spending: Great fortunes are often lost one dollar at time. It may not seem like a big deal when you pick up that double-mocha cappuccino, stop for a pack of cigarettes, have dinner out or order that pay-per-view movie, but every little item adds up. These personal habits often carry over to how we run our business and treat spending.

Organize Personal Finances

Organizing finances is the prelude to getting to a usable budget. You need to first understand your spending and earning habits before you can create a budget. Organizing your personal finances with the help of a qualified financial planner can be very useful.

Budgets

There are several tools available for creating a budget to track monthly expenses. For personal expenses, using something as simple as Mint.com or the tracking feature that most banks have available can quickly give you an insight into how much you are spending and where. What you are spending should not be the only consideration for a budget. However, you need to consider what you make and what you can afford. Putting those in perspective will help tremendously in determining a feasible budget.

Benefits of Working With a CPA

A CPA (or other qualified business accounting professional) is an important part of building and growing a business. Ensuring proactive tracking of income and expenses and clean financial reporting will give the business owner a wealth of information on operating their business. Also from a tax perspective planning and understanding your tax burdens so they don't creep up on you are extremely important as well.

Get Your Personal Finances in Order

Have a plan! Understand what running your business will entail financially and ensuring that your finances are in order prior to setting out on that journey will greatly enhance your ability to succeed.

Also, don't discount bartering as a way to increase revenues and decrease out of pocket cash expenses. And by bartering, I am referring to working through a trusted barter organization, not just exchanging services under the table. Barter organizations can help new business owners fill empty schedules with new sources of business and in the process create an income stream using a community currency that can be spent on a variety of services including accounting and bookkeeping. I have seen it work well for many of my clients and I have been an advocate and beneficiary of multiple barter networks over the past several years.

*****

FOR MY EYES ONLY

Isabel "Liz" Green, Ph.D. is a clinical psychologist in South Pasadena, California and has been in sole practice for more than 20 years counseling children, adolescents and adults.

In my field as a clinical psychologist, there are many of us that fit the classification of being sole proprietors. Rather than working in a hospital setting or at a medical complex, we have private offices, set our own hours, and schedule our own consultations and therapy sessions with our patients. My particular area of expertise is in working with children who are struggling to keep up in school and whose parents are often bewildered about why it's happening and where to turn for help. Understandably, the parental angst is sometimes compounded by fears that once a child has been tested and diagnosed, he or she will be labeled by society as having "something wrong" with them. Certainly many concerns warrant psychological testing such as issues with learning, attention, depression and anxiety. To be of the most value, my test protocols, interpretations and diagnoses must be accurate and precise in order to identify the nature of a disorder.

Because I'm not a part of a larger provider group, I personally administer and interpret all testing and I invest a great deal of time getting to know my clients in order to create an environment in which they can truly feel safe and secure. The worst thing in the world that could happen is if the dynamics of confidentiality and trust that I work so hard to build and maintain are compromised by someone who doesn't have my clients' best interests at heart.

For me, the weakest potential link in that chain of responsibility is a part-time office worker.

When you have a full caseload, there are only so many hours in a workday that you can attend to office housekeeping tasks such as editing reports, making photocopies, creating files, and preparing billing statements. While these are fairly routine clerical tasks that can be delegated to a student who wants to make some extra money, someone in my profession simply can't afford to have someone on the premises who doesn't know how to exercise an extremely high level of discretion.

No matter what type of business you run – but especially if it's one where clients have personal problems they've sought you out to help resolve – it's critical that you have The Talk with your clerical helpers before they ever start working for you. The purpose of this talk is to put the issue of confidentiality into a relatable context, that context being the profound hurt almost everyone has experienced in having a secret betrayed. Whether it's the best friend you told in elementary school "Don't tell anybody that I really like Bobby Holbrook" or the concerned neighbor to whom you tearfully confided over morning coffee "I don't know how Harry and I are going to be able to pay next month's rent," just imagine the embarrassment and anger of finding out that your supposedly sympathetic listener couldn't keep that exchange to herself. To borrow from the catchphrase about Las Vegas, what happens in my office *stays* in my office…and it's emphasized that rule continues even after they're no longer assisting me. As an added precaution, I also schedule my helpers' hours to be after work and/or on weekends so there is never any accidental contact with a client who is arriving or departing.

Unless your part-timers have a genuine interest in understanding your practice because it's a career they'd like to pursue themselves someday, many of them see their employment with you as little more than a paycheck and a revolving door to something better. In my experience, I've had temps who were either quite bright and capable but could never be relied on to show up when they were supposed to and others by whom I could practically set my watch and yet constantly had to correct a multiplicity of sloppy mistakes. Suffice it to say, neither scenario is acceptable to me, nor should it be to you if you have a vested interest in reputation management.

My work also requires me to be able to locate files quickly and with 100 percent assurance that their contents are fully up to date. The last thing I need is a temporary hire who lets things stack up, files materials in the wrong place, or – even worse – is tempted to read what's in them. A slip of the tongue to friends or relatives could set other tongues wagging in fairly short order; whether your business is in a small community or a large one, it's only a matter of time that word can get out you're not a faithful guardian of your clients' most privileged secrets.

*****

ENSURING/INSURING SUCCESSFUL OUTCOMES

Marti Masterson established Masterson Insurance Agency in October, 1996 in Northwest Indiana. She's sits on various boards including United Way of Porter County and Housing Opportunities and is an active Rotarian.

Every sole proprietor should have a professional liability policy also known as errors and omissions. Basically, it provides protection for your business services from claims of failing to perform your duties or claims of negligence. For example, if you're a hairstylist with a store front, your policy would protect you if someone trips inside or outside of your building. The same goes for business professionals with an office. If you rent, however, you'll have to show proof of insurance before anything would get to the landlord. Another example is a graphic designer. Instead of you being sued, a claim would be filed against your business.

A sole proprietor who has an eCommerce business needs insurance as well. Keep in mind that if you're shipping and delivering items, you'll want to make sure you're protected as damages may occur during shipping.

The type of insurance your need depends on your business. For example, if you own a restaurant, you'll want to have an insurance policy that covers spoilage (health) and things like that. If you're in an office, you'll want to consider if you back up your information and how secure is the information. Do you just have paper files? What happens if you have a fire? Make sure you have coverage for this. If you're a specialist, let's say a dentist, you'll want to have equipment coverage, such as tables, chairs, patient chairs, etc. An insurance policy must be tailored to your type of business.

Let's say you have a "cottage food" business. This is one where you make certain types of food from your home kitchen, then legally sell it at venues such as carnivals, craft shows, festivals and fairs. Before you ever start this type of business, you not only need to check with your city or state's department of health regarding licensing requirements but also allow your home kitchen to be open to regular – and often unannounced – inspections.

There are many insurance companies that don't like in-home businesses, especially those involving the preparation and sale of edible goods. This type of business is a tough one because of the number of rules governing it, coupled with even *more* rules relevant to online sales (eCommerce) and shipping. There is another insurance step that goes along with this. It's complicated, which is why you need to speak with a reputable insurance agent who can help you get the proper insurance you need. Let them educate you so that you and your business are protected.

I recently read a story about a sole proprietor wine maker who was growing grapes to make their own wine. They would go to different markets and give out their wine as samples. They did not check and did not do their homework to see if they needed any sort of license to do this. Accordingly, they ended up paying a $10,000 fine because they were in violation of existing rules.

Licensing is important. You'll want to check with your city, county and state as to what type of license you need for your business. This is easy to find out as most states have websites where a business owner can find out the licenses and professional certifications they need. An insurance agent isn't in charge of advising you on this topic; you'll need to do that legwork yourself.

If you have or want to have employees in your business, you'll need to have a workers' compensation policy. If you're using a car, truck or van to make deliveries, you'll need commercial and auto insurance policies. If you register as an LLC or Sub S Corporation and register your vehicle under the business name, you'll receive a nice tax break.

It's best for a sole proprietor to become an LLC or incorporate, so that you can take advantage of the protection these designations offer. An LLC or Sub S Corporation becomes a wall of defense for your business. For example, let's say you're an electrician and did wiring on an addition to a house. A year later there was a fire and the cause was because of something electrical in the addition. The owner of the house would go after the electrician, sole proprietor. Hopefully, the electrician would have at least a business owner's or contractor's policy for liability. But if there were any injuries, loss of use or trauma, the home owner could sue the sole proprietor as well as the insurance carrier.

Unfortunately, we live in a very litigious society. Here's an example of a sole proprietor who learned the hard way about not enforcing tenants to purchase renters' insurance:

An owner of a four-plex rental building called for insurance because his company did not renew his policy. It was a situation where he required tenants to carry their own renters' insurance, but he did not enforce the rule. One of the tenants fell on some steps and is suing the building owner for medical.

Here's another one about a friend who hired his friend to do work because he was out of a job and wanted to help him out:

A friend of mine performed excavation work. A friend of his was out of a job and, to help him out, my friend let him do work, and was paid cash under the table. A piece of machinery hit him in the head. He became a paraplegic due to the accident. The friend was sued, as well as the insurance carrier.

People think, "Oh. They're so nice, they won't sue me." Guess what? The reality is when something happens, you may get sued. This is why it's important for a sole proprietor to purchase insurance from a licensed agent. Insurance certifications look good on paper, and there are some agents who are just order-takers. They're focused on making money, not helping a sole proprietor get the proper insurance and coverage.

Before you select an insurance agent, Google insurance agencies and read reviews. It's best to find a local agent whom you can build and develop a business relationship with over the long-term. Also, check with your state's Department of Insurance. They will show you, usually online, whether an agent has had disciplinary problems. If you have a claim, you can easily contact your agent and discuss your situation. Work with and hire an insurance agent that cares about you and your sole proprietorship.

It begs reiterating that every sole proprietor would benefit from getting the proper business insurance for their business. You should also look into the various licenses and permits you may need to properly run your business, especially if you're operating a cottage food business.

Whether you use contracts is up to you and depends on your chosen industry and whether you provide goods or services. For example, if you own a graphic design/printing company, you may not have a contract with each and every one of your customers. However, if the work you're performing is on a larger scale, you may have a contract with a customer.

There are a number of websites where you can download sample contracts and templates. While not mandatory, it's recommended that you hire an attorney to draw up any contract you may need or at least have him/her review yours. This will help ensure that all bases have been covered with clarity and efficiency.

IF YOU BUILD IT, THEY MAY
(OR MAY NOT) COME

If a man has good corn or wood, or boards, or pigs, to sell, or can make better chairs or knives, crucibles or church organs, than anybody else, you will find a broad hard-beaten road to his house, though it be in the woods.

This quote by Ralph Waldo Emerson is perhaps better known by its short, paraphrased version: *Build a better mousetrap, and the world will beat a path to your door.*

Whether your product is mousetraps, cupcakes or novels, however, getting the world to actually discover its existence takes more than random luck and word-of-mouth. Among the many hats you'll don when you become a sole proprietor is that of a marketing professional with tireless energy, exceptional communication skills, and a lot of imagination.

None of this stops, either, once customers start coming in your door. From that point – and ever after – you need to hang on to them and keep them excited by expanding your scope of products/services, experimenting with new marketing techniques, rewarding customers for their loyalty, and taking maximum advantage of all the social media tools available to you.

When your marketing budget is tight, your focus on what works and what doesn't has to be even tighter. Not only must you know what kind of client you want to attract but also what circles these individuals are already traveling in to find what your own business wants to sell.

To reverse engineer this concept for a moment, start paying attention to the types of commercials that air during your favorite television programs or on the radio during your daily commute. During a sports program, for instance, you're not going to find ads for cleaning products, diapers, or cosmetics because none of these are of any interest to the sports program's demographic: males. Instead, you'll find one commercial after another for cars, trucks, junk food, beer and "performance" supplements. On the daily commute, radio ads usually focus on cars that get better mileage (than whatever they're currently driving), all-inclusive cruises (to remind drivers they need a vacation), family fun (to remind them they have a life outside of work), and fast-food (to subliminally make them seek out the nearest drive-through).

What you can learn from this and apply to your customer-seeking strategy is that before you spend a lot of money on print or electronic advertising, brochures, flyers, or pricey mailing lists, make sure it's going to reach the audience you want and that they'll be amenable to your call to action.

*****

WHO'S YOUR DREAM CLIENT?

Anthony Kirlew is a serial entrepreneur and digital marketing expert. Since 1999, he has helped countless companies and organizations improve their online presence and increase their bottom line revenues.

It's important for sole proprietors to know who their ideal clients are. Why? Because identifying the ideal client makes it easier for that client to find you.

For example, if your tagline is "We help dentists grow their business online" then that message would resonate with your ideal client, who you have identified as a dentist. Once you have identified this client, your job should go more smoothly because you are prepared for them, you understand their needs, and speak their language.

If you haven't identified your ideal client, you may end up frustrated and wondering why you end up with such a wide range of stressful client engagements. You may also have a hard time finding them because you won't have a specific "target" in mind. From a referral stand point, it will be harder to articulate to others who may be in a position to refer new business to you, *what* type of client you are looking for.

In the end, identifying the ideal client will save you lots of time in prospecting and you don't waste your time or theirs. Also, the more niche your ideal client is, the better off the business will do because experts typically get paid more, and you will be developing expertise around your ideal client.

If you don't know who your ideal client is you may

waste lots of time by either serving a client who cannot pay you what you are worth, or the spend time with a prospective client whose needs far exceed the expertise needed by you, the sole proprietor. In the end, your business becomes very inefficient.

Defining and Finding Clients

When I started my online marketing company, I was like many business owners and thought that "everyone was a prospect." I learned over time that there are industries that I can relate to well and others where it's a stretch. If I am familiar with the industry and client type, it's smoother all around for everyone and in the end a more successful campaign.

We did not have social media and that has become a big source of prospects for me. Secondly, networking is a skill that most new entrepreneurs don't have. It's something that I have developed over time and now have a passion for. Lastly is speaking and presenting workshops. Public speaking is one of those things that many people are not comfortable with. I have had great success in having people interested in my business offering after hearing me speak. My philosophy is to educate – not sell. If people see the need and believe I can help them after hearing me speak, they will contact me. I just like to treat people as I like to be treated. I attend seminars and workshops to be educated, not sold to.

As a new business owner, it's understandable that one would also be afraid to get in front of an audience and say the wrong thing. For those who want to improve those skills, I recommend Toastmasters, which is a great organization that helps business owners become expert communicators. As a former Toastmaster, I can highly recommend it.

To find your ideal client, consider the following:

- Ask yourself what problems you solve, and who you have had the best success solving them for.
- Ask yourself what kinds of clients you enjoy working with (assuming you have already started the business)

To me, the winning combination is serving clients, while making money and having fun all at the same time. Whether you ask for referrals or join networking groups, there are many ways sole proprietors can find their ideal clients. Listed below are some of the most effective ways to find them.

Ask for Referrals

Start with people you know and tell them the kind of client you are looking for (your ideal client) and ask them for a name and phone number of someone you can call, using them as a reference. If you are feeling bold, ask for two or more names.

Networking Groups

There are lots of networking groups, and the prices range from free to a few hundred dollars per year. My strong advice in these situations is to be an educator, not someone who is always pitching your business. Don't always pitch to the people in the group; ask them who they know who might be a fit, based on who your ideal client is (i.e. "I serve small businesses who don't have a web presence. I typically offer a free website analysis to prospects, and I was curious to know if you could you refer me to two local business owners that I could offer this free analysis to?"). What often happens when you make an offer like that, the person might have the same need and ask if you can help them, but this way you didn't come across as simply selling to them.

Chambers of Commerce

Joining a Chamber of Commerce is a great way to connect with other like-minded business owners to network. In my experience, it's also a great way to get involved in the community and connect with community and political leaders. I will say this; just joining won't give you much benefit. You need to get involved, attend the meetings, and serve on a committee, so that others (in particular the leadership) gets to know who you are and feel comfortable referring customers to your business.

Teach a Class

This is a great way to connect with your ideal client and also to have people see you as the expert that you are. Ask those in leadership at your Chamber of Commerce of networking group if you can present a workshop on the topic of your expertise.

LinkedIn

LinkedIn is the number one professional social network to find people who need your service. A few keys to success on LinkedIn are:

- Have a complete profile with a photo. This will allow people to get to know you before reaching out to you.
- Post some content. Just like the case with offline networking, you want to be seen as an educator. When you post, be cautious of posting offers or "selling" as that just isn't the place for that.

Facebook

This is a great place to connect with those you know, and they can be a great source of referrals if they know what you do. Become the educator in your field to your friends and family, but also make sure to balance "business" posts with personal posts on your personal timeline. Launching a Facebook business page is a great way to separate business posts from personal posts, and a great way to get additional exposure for the business without feeling like you are giving up the privacy of your personal Facebook timeline.

Cold Calling

I am sure you just had a reaction…and probably not a good one! Many people don't like cold calling, but I have a saying "in business, the phone has to ring, and if others aren't making your phone ring, you need to make their phone ring." I call this "dialing for dollars" and I never recommend any strategy that I have not used myself. In a day and age where we have so much technology, you might think "why cold call?" The answer is that it works. In fact, when you have identified your ideal client and can let someone know you are an expert in their industry, it works even better. It is not something you need to do long-term, but it's a great way to kick off a business. As you find clients and do great work for them, they will become your advocates and send you referrals. And that's how you turn cold calls into warm calls. You do need to be aware that in your area there may be certain laws you need to comply with, so check that before diving in.

One of my entrepreneurial pursuits was real estate. When I was a young real estate agent, I would lock myself in an office, get out the Haines Criss+Cross Directory and start dialing. This was a book that had every house listed by street and it listed the home owner and the phone number. I got to enjoy the phones and made it a game. In the end, I made quite a bit of money cold calling, and on more than one occasion.

If you are considering cold calling, I will say that you should make sure that the value of the customer justifies the time. In the real estate business when you are earning commissions in the several thousand dollar range, it's clearly worth it. If you are selling cell phone covers, it might not be a good investment of time.

Collaboration

I have to thank one of my business coaches (Kyle Morgan) for this one. Collaboration refers to building a trusted network based on alignment of core values and common goals. In a collaborative community, you can actually work with other businesses that do the exact same thing and serve the exact same client. You don't see them as competition; you see them as "co-opetition". Collaboration can lead to much more business than you could produce on your own, and most people would be surprised at how effective it is.

I built a very successful Internet marketing company during a down economy and this was one of our primary strategies. It keeps business costs down due to shared resources and keeps marketing costs down because it generates new business opportunities that have a higher success rate that most other forms of marketing.

Internet and Social Media

In addition to the above techniques for finding clients, sole proprietors can use the Internet and social media to attract and find their ideal clients.

First, have a website. Make sure it is optimized to reach those who are searching for the business in the search engines (and mobile friendly). It's critical to have a website no matter how simple.

If you can't afford a professional website, then something is always better than nothing. Make sure the website has your contact information on it, and ideally a way for them to want to connect with you (i.e., give me your email and I will send you a free ebook.) The more opportunities you give for prospects to interact, the more they will take you up on it.

Ideally, the website will have a blog so you can share lots of tips with your prospects. This is also the content you will share via social media, and the search engines will gladly index it and share it with other searching for your business.

As far as social media goes, I recommend a three part strategy:

- **Create (your social media profiles).** Start with LinkedIn, Facebook, and Twitter, and on LinkedIn and Facebook, make sure to also create the appropriate page for your business.
- **Connect.** Build a community of fans and followers starting with those you know first. Those who know you will come on board faster than someone who does not know you. As you build this audience, you can educate them over time by sharing your expertise; and sharing your blog content is a great strategy for educating your audience.
- **Communicate.** Share your insights and expertise with your social networks. When people ask questions, turn it into a blog post and then share it with everyone because chances are more than one person has the same question.

Firing and Outgrowing Clients

Sometimes, you have to fire clients. While you may not want to let go of a client, it may necessary for the growth of your business. For example, I've had to fire a client. This client had expectations that were simply too high. Specifically, they wanted sushi on a fast food budget. It's not always easy to have those conversations, but in this case I explained why it was not a good fit. I told them I wanted them to have the best service and that there was probably a better provider for them. I even went out and found a new provider for them. Incidentally, this seemed to reduce the client's demands, but I still stuck to my guns and ended the relationship.

When starting out, we often make the mistake of identifying our target client at a lower price point than we desire. This is often based on a few factors, but I'd say a common theme is undervaluing our service. The challenge is that once we gain that confidence and start to charge full price, we are stuck with unprofitable client relationships and it's hard to raise the price incrementally enough times to make it profitable.

Another factor is that we grow over time, so we may end up finding that a certain niche (it could be an industry or a service offering) is a great fit for our business and then we need to make a shift in that direction.

In my opinion, you never want to abandon those clients who entrusted their business to you as you were growing. In some cases, you can maintain them as you grow, but in other cases, it becomes evident that you need to help them transition to a new provider. Finding a strategic (collaboration) partner can be a great solution. In fact, the right partner might even pay you an ongoing referral fee for the business and, again, everyone wins.

Keep Clients Coming Back

As a sole proprietor, it's important to retain clients – make them want to be loyal to you. You must make people feel valued as customers. I have a saying and that is, "I don't want to gain a new client at the expense of a current client." Stay in touch with your clients and ask them specific questions so you know how happy they are with your service. Make sure you have defined the goals that will determine what a successful outcome is.

A periodic thank-you call or handwritten letter is that extra touch that lets people know you care. And above all, make sure you give amazing customer service. If you employ an assistant make sure he or she understands the value of customer service and how crucial it is that your customers are treated like royalty.

Overcome Obstacles to Finding Ideal Clients

It's important to realize that most sole proprietors face obstacles. For example, as a young real estate agent, I faced early obstacles, one of which was being young and not having a network of people who were in the home buyer demographic. To overcome these obstacles, I pursued lots of marketing avenues such as flyer, ads, and even cold calls. I didn't have the Internet (it was 1992), so today, things would be much different.

Later obstacles I had to overcome occurred when I started my first online marketing firm (1999). It was at a time where it was such a new space, so there were lots of clients for me as a solopreneur. All I had to do was mention what I did and people were lining up. The growth challenges came as I took on partners and we had a "real business" and needed to ramp up and get enough clients to ensure we all got paid. A few lessons I learned (based on the latter experience) were:

- It's really important to pick the right partners; it's like a marriage and thankfully, I was blessed with some great partners.
- Systems are really important. Having lots of leads is not fun if you don't have a system to nurture them. It makes you seem unreliable or flaky if you don't get back to people in a timely manner and losing prospective clients is not something a new business can afford.
- Unless you are an accountant, an accountant will be one of your best friends. If you are spending time pulling your hair out doing something you dislike (such as accounting), it will drain your energy and you won't be as effective as you could be with the rest of your business.

- If you discount your services to build your business, you will never get those clients to pay your actual rates.

The Sole Proprietor's Toobox

There are two tools that every business owner, no matter how small, should be using:

- A Customer Relationship Management (CRM) tool

  This will allow you to track and follow up with leads. It's important to do this because the longer time period you allow between contacts, the less likely that person is going to do business with you. A great system for new entrepreneurs is Insightly. It's free for up to 3 users, so you can't beat that.

- An Email Marketing System

  A good system will allow you to collect email addresses from your website, send automated email responses, and allow you to send periodic email updates and electronic newsletters. I recommend AWeber, which I have used for years. You can try the first month for just $1 then it starts at $19 per month. It's money well spent because you need to communicate with your prospects and clients and using your personal email is not recommended as it is often out of compliance with Federal and local anti-spam laws.

Go Forth and Define and Find Your Ideal Clients

Put the time in to find your ideal clients. Find out what problem they have that needs solving and how you can help them. The more time you spend on this step, the easier it will be to find your ideal clients and market to them.

MEETS AND GREETS

If a magician explained in advance all the detailed mechanics of a particular trick, would there still be a reason to stay for the actual performance? Arguably, there are those who might steal the trick once they saw how it was done and shamelessly stitch it into their own repertoire. On the flip side are those who would not only respect the magician's craft but might also think, "If I could be that wowed seeing one illusion, I wonder what else this guy has up his sleeve!"

A correlation can be made to the wizardry of a sole proprietor offering professional consulting, advertising design, and wordsmithing. Specifically, it's a common practice in these industries to offer a free consultation, the purpose of which is to identify a prospective client's needs, demonstrate one's expertise to address those needs, and determine whether the respective personalities are a smart fit. The highest chance of such meetings failing to seal the deal is when the person making the pitch presupposes a level of loyalty that has yet to be forged and, thus, reveals all the tricks of the trade at the initial meeting. "You've certainly given me a lot to think about," the listener says, not the least of which is now whether they need to hire an expert at all.

I recently interviewed a potential ghostwriting client who wanted to hire me to pen her screenplay idea about an obscure Italian painter. Starting her story in the wrong place and not giving her protagonist any compelling conflicts were just two of the problems inherent in this project; she had also put no thought into who its target market was. These things could be remedied, I suggested, if it were developed as a stage play instead of a movie. The intimate, real-time bond the actors could make with the audience would invite a deeper understanding of what fueled the artist's passions and relationships with others. In response to her assertion that theater was too limiting for all the scenes she wanted, I pointed out that elements such as selective lighting, scrim curtains, platforms, stairs, and holograms could deliver far more visual variety than she thought. Further, theater patrons typically process information at a higher level of abstraction than movie goers; i.e., you can tell them a minimalist stage is a dense forest and they'll "see" it without your having to bring on a single tree.

By the end of the consultation, she was excited but wanted to make her decision the following week. When she did, it was to inform me that – despite her lack of any playwriting experience – she was going to write the whole script herself rather than pay someone who had obviously divulged "everything about theater there is to know."

Or did I?

Her belief that she had tricked me into giving her something-for-nothing was only an illusion. The reality – the portion of the iceberg not visible from the surface – is what I could have shown her about how to keep an audience spellbound.

*****

FIRST AND LAST(ING) IMPRESSIONS

Author, editor, publisher and radio host Tony Wilkins is the owner of TCS Inc., a business development consulting firm specializing in cold calling, sales and marketing consulting and training for over 30 years.

We've all been there. You get a call or e-mail from a prospective client requesting a meeting to discuss your services. Naturally you're excited to put your best foot forward; but like many new business owners you may let your enthusiasm get in the way of "wowing" the prospect. Here's what I do to prepare for any meeting....

Before the Meeting....

The first thing I do to prepare for an initial meeting with a prospect is to visit the prospect's site. The site can tell me a number of things about my future client. For example, if the site looks thrown together or cheap; chances are they aren't spending a lot on outside services. I'd also want to know how long they've been in business, how many employees they have and who the key players in the firm are. The site will also tell me about their customer base and if the firm is part of a larger corporation or chain. Going directly to the firm's site is one of the best ways to understand who they are and what they do and who I'm dealing with.

Another rule of thumb is to check out their Linkedin.com profile. Do they have endorsements from others? Do we have connections in common? For me it's about finding a common link with the prospect before the meeting. Knowledge of forethought is a powerful tool.

I next Google the name of the contact as well as the company itself. This tactic will tell me several things including if the firm or its key players have made news, if they have any customer reviews (or complaints) and if it's a well established firm.

Does the firm have many competitors? Are they local? Knowing a bit about their industry helps me to understand the best way to help them.

Be sure to confirm the day before the meeting via e-mail. I also want to get directions, taxi information etc. to ensure that that unexpected mishaps are kept to a minimum (i.e. no public transit after 5pm).

I prefer to arrive a good 20 minutes early (for any meeting) just in case there's traffic, but mostly to get centered before the meeting. Arriving frazzled, sweaty and out of breath sends a bad message to the prospect and makes me look unprepared.

During the Meeting...

It's the day of the meeting and I've done my research. Here's my plan for ensuring its success....

They say that you never have a second chance to make a first impression and that's true. And while I no longer wear a suit and tie to every meeting, I do dress for the occasion and the audience. Perhaps it's age or the fact that I've been in business for over 30 years, but I find that casual elegance goes a long way to showing the client who I am. As an independent contractor, I can usually get away with a nice sports jacket, slacks and dress shirt without looking like I'm going on my first job interview. And while I'm on the subject of fashion, leave the cologne at home. I love wearing cologne but not everyone wants my scent left in their office long after I've gone.

While a good handshake and eye contact go a long way to projecting a positive image, what really shows me a person is a professional is if they have business cards on hand for the meeting. This sounds like such a simple thing, but I can't tell you the number of professionals that don't bother to bring them. To me, the lack of having a simple card is a signal that they aren't prepared to do business.

If I really want to get more information out of a prospect I utilize the "interviewer's trick" by asking questions. Open ended questions are a great way to keep the dialogue going and learn more about the firm and the client's needs. Here are some examples:

- "How soon will you need help with this project?"
- "Have you worked with a similar firm before?"
- "Tell me about that experience".
- "What do you want to accomplish with this project?"

Asking these questions is a great way to determine the client's needs, because if there's no need then there's no sale.

After the Meeting...

There are several meeting etiquette rules that I adhere to for after the meeting:

- A follow up phone call or e-mail the day after the meeting (thanking them for their time) is perfectly acceptable (and in fact it's expected). I then ask if the prospect would like a follow up call to close the deal or at the very least if they have some thoughts on a submitted quote.
- If the prospect has given a follow-up date and time, be sure to adhere to it. You're at the finish line. Don't be afraid to cross it. In other words, ask for the order.
- The prospect may be on the fence in terms of retaining my services so I query how I can get their business which is a great way to determine the reason behind their reluctance. After all, if I don't ask the question, how will I know how to close them?
- Deliver what you promised. Not every project works out but now that you've got the project it's up to you to make sure the client is happy.

The bottom line is that each meeting is an opportunity to close the deal. By simply following these basic meeting rules, you'll increase your closing ratio exponentially.

*****

WELCOME TO YOUR VIRTUAL COCKTAIL PARTY

Shari Stauch, creator of Where Writers Win, has been involved in publishing and marketing for 30 years, first for individual athletes, and now for authorpreneurs.

"Life's Just a Cocktail Party..." – Mick Jagger, "Shattered"

In today's virtual world, the advantages of a professional online presence cannot be overstated: It's easier to drill down to find your ready-made customer base. It's inexpensive to maintain an online presence through social media engagement and blogging. And it's useful to receive fast feedback from customers and fans on everything from your latest product to your new marketing campaign.

Learning to engage the "right" way in this brave new digital world is just as important as engaging someone live. You'll want to develop a written voice that's casual yet professional, enticing yet not too wordy.

In short, your virtual interactions are much like any networking cocktail party, but in print.

Ah, but unlike the live cocktail party, you don't need to dress up or wear uncomfortable shoes. You won't need to fill the tank or grab a taxi, travel across town or across the country. You won't have to wander the room, looking for others with the same interests as you, hoping to catch them before they leave. You won't even need to buy a drink!

Working the virtual room is like working any room. Specifically:

- You go in not knowing many people, and hug the wall a bit until you get your bearings. In the virtual world, that means joining groups on LinkedIn or Facebook, then watching the discussions until you're ready to join in with a well-placed comment of your own.
- You introduce yourself, get introduced to others, and have the good sense to ask those you "meet" about what they're up to.
- Soon you'll be confident enough to introduce others; getting known as a connector is a bonus no matter your business.

- As you get to know the people you meet, you'll share other things besides what you "do." That can include photos of the ski vacation, a great restaurant recommendation, a good read, whatever you can share that will help you foster *closer connections*, whether they're down the block or across the ocean.

All this fun does come with a surgeon general's warning: What you wouldn't do at a live party (unless you want to send the people you meet scurrying to refill their drinks) is shout your presence and talk to everyone you meet as if you were on stage and they paid to see you perform. They didn't. The same rules apply online.

The other big no-no at the virtual party is the "I must be right" argument. At a live party, you have the advantage of verbal and visual cues that will tell you perhaps you should stop yammering. But the only cue you'll get online is that people will stop engaging with you, un-follow you, or, in extreme cases, block you.

In this way, the online community is often considered a kinder, gentler form of marketing, but infinitely more powerful. Rather than shouting your message or making outrageous claims that your product or service is the *best*, you're *inviting* people to give it/you a try. Then you're inviting them –if they like it/you– to tell their friends to give it/you a try. In this way you're building a tribe of loyal followers, all of whom can be an extension of your solo marketing efforts. Suddenly, you have a team!

So how do you use the virtual party to your best benefit? Once you've established which online parties you'd like to frequent (meaning the social networks populated by your customers/fans and the groups visited by your clients and peers), you can use your online power to help achieve all your business goals.

This typically involves a multi-faceted approach to your online strategy. In example, here are several ways I've used online engagement to grow my own business:

1. **Finding/sourcing other "team" members.** These have included interns, experts wanting another platform to share their own expertise, and any trusted resource to whom I can refer clients with confidence for services outside what I provide. Even if you're a one-person shop, you can

surround yourself with a virtual team. And by referring clients, I receive a great many referrals in return.

2. **Feedback.** Soliciting feedback from clients includes requesting comments on blog posts, conducting surveys to learn what clients want to learn, and asking questions about the services we provide and how we can do better. Customers love to weigh in and feel like they're part of the planning process, and their input is always valuable. Clients also offer feedback in the form of testimonials, which creates more referrals.

3. **Expanding knowledge.** If I don't have an answer, I now have access to a wealth of experts just clicks away that *will* have the answer. Talk about being able to stay responsive to customers with accurate information! And I expect our readers would soon tire of just reading my point of view all the time, so I also invite guest bloggers to share their expertise, offering readers more knowledge than I could hope to provide.

4. **Know your competition.** I can quickly discover what others are charging for similar services, and what services they're providing, to allow me to decide how to make our services unique, and stay competitive. *But also do seek to engage with competitors!* I've formed wonderful, productive relationships with other author service providers. We all learn from each other so we can each better serve our own client base.

5. **Building reputation.** By doing all of the above and interacting in various groups and forums, it's easy to rather quickly establish yourself as a credible expert in your field, something that might take years to accomplish in the live arena.

6. **Lead generation.** Finally, yes, there are sales to be had online, or at least leads that will produce sales. But notice that I listed this point last. If you're using your online presence for all your other goals, this one is just a natural byproduct!

I look forward to meeting you at the world's biggest cocktail party; do stop by and introduce yourself. Who knows what connections we can make together!

*****

EVENT CENTRAL

Serial entrepreneur and online marketing expert John Leo Weber is Head of SEO for Geek Powered Studios in Austin, Texas.

As a one-person enterprise, orchestrating an "event" of any size is probably the farthest thing from your mind. And yet with some imagination and the right networking, an event can be an effective way to put your sole proprietorship in the spotlight.

Over the years, I've booked and promoted thousands of events in 46 of the 50 United States. Most of these were concerts (in my music industry days) but I've also had the pleasure of putting together workshops, speaking engagements, and marketing classes for numerous small businesses. I've learned that planning an event for a small business can be a pain - as it often requires lots of legwork upfront - but events typically pay off in the form of new relationships, press recognition, and even new clients.

For sole proprietors with little experience in event planning, I'd encourage you to start by putting together a free event where you can teach people in your community something about your trade. If you do crafts and jewelry, for example, you could put on a free jewelry-making class. If you're in marketing like I am, you could give a short class on using social media to grow a business.

The secret to making these events a success is to give enough useful information to your audience without eliminating them from your potential customer pool (and creating competitors for yourself!) You can show or teach a few simple, easy-to-learn techniques to tease the interest of your students but leave your signature products and methods a secret. By holding some information back, you open the door to upsell your students who wish to learn more. This is similar to the classic self-help seminars that are free to attend but to "unlock" the full package students need to pay for additional services. Most times, offering a free class will turn into enough sales to cover your costs, not to mention the valuable relationships you'll build in your industry and your community.

As you plan bigger and bigger events, you'll see your costs and planning needs increase. I've put together some simple tips that hopefully you can use in putting together your next small business event, whether it be free or paid.

Find The Right Venue

Finding the perfect venue isn't always easy so I'd suggest that you start contacting rooms at least six months ahead of your event date. Don't be afraid to get creative with venues - oftentimes coffee shops, churches, hotels, and theaters have meeting rooms available for rent. If you need ideas on where to host your event, try reaching out to a local promoter who is familiar with the scene in your town. Promoters have their ears to the ground when it comes to events, and can often suggest venues you might have not even considered.

Most venues book 3-4 months out so getting in early will give you a better chance at securing your first choice. Contact a variety of venues and ask to put your target date on "hold." This means you'll be penciled into the calendar tentatively until the details are hashed out. Oftentimes I will put 3-4 venues on hold at the same time and leverage the venues against one another to get the best deal. Once you secure a venue, however, don't forget to "release" your holds at the other rooms so you're not wasting dates that other people can use.

Negotiate!

Just like in car buying, room rentals and fees are almost always negotiable. Don't be afraid to ask for lower rates or waived fees, especially if your event is for a non-profit. If your event is going to be a paid and ticketed event, a great way to save money upfront is to ask the venue for a "door deal." This means that instead of paying a hefty rental fee to secure the room upfront, you would instead split the profits with the venue immediately after the event. A standard split is anywhere from 90% /10% (you /venue) to 60/ 40%. With a door deal, you can avoid having to cut a check before the event's profits come in. This also puts some of the promotion burden onto the venue; the more tickets sold, the more money the venue makes.

Don't Go Out of Pocket

There are always ways to avoid upfront expenses, with the most important method being sponsorship. About 4-9 months in advance of your event, you should start seeking sponsorship dollars, as many companies plan their marketing budgets on an annual or quarterly basis. There are plenty of companies out there eager to throw money or in-kind products at events in order to get their logo in front of a large audience. Getting sponsorships to cover your expenses is a numbers game so don't be afraid to ask! Make sure to have a sponsorship deck ready to show potential sponsoring companies so they can see what, exactly, they'll be getting for their money.

Promote For Cheap

Don't make the mistake of blowing your entire budget on printing posters or hiring a publicist. There are several ways to promote for cheap instead:

- Use your existing social media networks. In many cases, your personal pages can actually be more useful than a company page, as your colleagues are more inclined to trust (and care about) things that come directly from you.
- Even if your event is free, get a ticketing company. Offering physical tickets to your event provides a level of authority and exclusivity that can add to the overall success of the event. I like to use companies like Brown Paper Tickets, as they're very reasonable in price (they just take a small percentage of every ticket sold) and because they have tools in place to help you promote. With Brown Paper Tickets, for example, their system will automatically submit your event to local newspapers and journalists to help get the word out (for free!) This can help to generate buzz around your event and will also get you listed on local events calendars around town.
- Don't forget to bother your friends. Word of mouth can go a long way for event publicity, and your friends and colleagues will be your best tool. Keep them in the

loop via phone calls and email and remind them often; people are busy and will forget if you're not persistent.

Planning a business event can seem daunting in terms of how much time and money you will likely spend, especially if you're a one-person office and already juggling multiple priorities. If done right, however, you'll see huge benefits for the bottom line of your company. Through planning these events, you'll meet other important people who can become valuable colleagues and customers, and develop yourself as an authority in your industry.

*****

HOW NOT TO WORK A ROOM

Flo Selfman is a longtime PR consultant for literary and entertainment clients; a proofreader-copyeditor; and president of Independent Writers of Southern California.

By definition, "network" is a group of people who keep in contact to exchange information. In other words, NET=WORK. According to networking expert Hank Blank, 74% of all jobs are found through networking and 75% of all business deals come from networking, yet most people don't know *how* to network.

As sole proprietors, especially those working from a home office, every opportunity to make connections and enhance our reputations is critical. It's easy to just "let our fingers do the walking" but it doesn't take the place of face-to-face contact. We need to create relationships.
Sometimes, though, we're so desperate to get "out there" that we sabotage our chances of being successful before we've even walked through the door.

We've all seen – or been – that person who arrives a half hour late to an event, out of breath, full of excuses, juggling purse, jacket, keys, business cards, plopping everything down on the nearest table and heading for the bar and food table. Food drops off her overloaded plate. She's oblivious to the eye-rolling around her as she spills wine (red wine! Doesn't she know that white looks so much better if you have to "wear" it?) while trying to retrieve her business cards from the depths of her handbag. Finally she extends a hand – and it's greasy.

If you want to reduce your chances of making business and social events work for you, just follow these easy steps!

1. Arrive late.
2. Hang around the bar. Eat or drink too much.
3. Sit with people you know.
4. Don't have business cards or copies of your book with you; or...
5. Have business cards deep inside your purse or in the car, not in your pocket or hand, and don't bother wearing a name tag.
6. Have a limp handshake.
7. Talk only about yourself and your business or book.
8. When asked, "What do you do?" or "What is your book about?" give a twenty-minute sales pitch.
9. Break into an ongoing conversation.
10. Spend all your time talking to someone who can't help you or isn't interested in you or your business.
11. If someone offers you a breath mint, say, "No, thanks."
12. Send a follow-up note and misspell the person's name or use an incorrect title.

Seriously, it's so easy to just run out the door and hope for the best. But with some advance planning, working the room can bring benefits to you and the people you meet. Whether the "room" is an elevator, conference, or chamber mixer, it can be a chance to shine.

Before the Event:

• Create and rehearse your 30-second "elevator speech."
• Prepare your wardrobe, including comfortable shoes; schedule any salon appointments; car wash and gas. Easy on the perfume or aftershave. Have credit card and cash, business cards, mints.
• Plan your route, giving enough time to arrive early. Allow for rush hour, crowding parking garages, slow elevators, and walking to the event location.
• *If you're early, you're on time, and if you're on time, you're late.* Being among the first to show up allows you to locate the restroom, freshen up, get your business cards out,

take a few deep breaths, and get a feeling for the room. Greeting people one at a time lets you "own" the event.

- Don't just collect business cards, have an objective: I will talk to five strangers. Or, I will set up one lunch meeting. It becomes easier to talk to people once you have a defined purpose.
- If you know an important person will be there, plan a question for him/her in advance so you won't get tongue-tied and miss the opportunity.

At the Event:

- Place your own business cards in your right-hand pocket for easy access. Put those you collect in your left-hand pocket after jotting a note on the back.
- Wear your name tag on your right side; when shaking hands, the eye follows your arm up to your name tag, reinforcing name and face. Write your first name in large letters; include last name and company, if there's room.
- How is your handshake? Be neither a bone-crusher nor a butterfly. If necessary, use a clear antiperspirant on sweaty palms or research a natural remedy.
- Don't overeat or overdrink, and choose wisely. You don't want to blow "Chablis breath" in someone's face. Do use good manners when eating in public. Don't get a negative reputation centered around food or alcohol.
- Be *interested in* others; be *interesting to* others. Don't monopolize the conversation. Don't interrupt people who are clearly engrossed in conversation; wait for an appropriate break before speaking. Don't spend too much time with one person; arrange to meet if he or she seems like a good business relationship prospect. If you came with a friend, split up and you can meet twice as many people. If it's a sit-down event, don't sit together.
- Don't sell. Give information and resources. *Selling inhibits a relationship. Networking bonds a relationship* – Melvin Kaufmann, *The Millionaire's Handbook.* If someone asks what you do, give the 30-second answer. If they want to know more, they'll ask. Then you can continue the conversation later and move on to someone else.

- Make eye contact and smile!

After the Event:

You're not done yet! Read on:

- Put your own materials away and file or toss any that you collected at the event.
- Enter relevant business card information into your database.
- Send a thank-you email to the hosts.
- If you promised information (not necessarily about your business), send it now.
- Set up meetings.
- Send "friend" requests – but don't add people to your lists without permission.
- And, please: *Respect people's privacy and always send blast emails as "bcc,"* never "to" or "cc."

Now, go forth and network!

HELP WANTED

Back in the days when I worked in state government, I always viewed summer with a mixed sense of anticipation and dread. Summer was the season of interns, the season when the floodgates would open and spill forth dozens of cattle-call applicants in their late teens and early twenties. Although these positions were unpaid, it was management's vision of a win/win scenario: the interns would get work experience to put on their resumes and the rest of us would get a cadre of malleable minions to do the filing, open mail, stock supplies, and run errands.

While now and again we'd delight in finding a true gem who had the skill sets, initiative, and leadership qualities that could one day translate to a full-time job with us, the majority of them were clearly not the sharpest knives in the drawer. Among them:

- The one who threw out any mail that personally didn't look interesting to her. (She asked me why we never got fashion magazines or *People*.)
- The one who filed all the travel claims under "S" for "someone who took a trip."
- The one who took over an hour to deliver a file to an office located on the same floor. (If we had traced his footprints, they would have looked like Billy's from a *Family Circus* cartoon.)

As the saying goes, good help is hard to find. Bad help (which is worse than no help at all) can take years off your life, cause costly mistakes and jeopardize your reputation. While government agencies and nonprofits have no problem doing shout-outs for extra pairs of hands, a lot of sole proprietors I've known over the years are not as willing to admit they're getting overwhelmed. A part of it, I think, is that they want to maintain the image they're completely in control (albeit exhausted to the point of collapse). They're also cognizant of the reality that in the length of time it takes to train a helper how to do something – or correct how the helper did it totally wrong – they could easily have just done it themselves.

Whether you're looking to go the intern route for short-term projects or planning to one day expand your sole proprietorship and put out the call for prospective employees, it's critical to have a clear sense of what you want, how much supervision you want/need to provide, and what the participants can potentially gain from the experience of working with you. The more "ownership" they feel they have in the process and the outcome, the more pride they'll take in paying attention and doing their assignments well.

These same elements apply to situations where you're subcontracting with local vendors to provide services (i.e., catering) or outsourcing product-oriented tasks (i.e., assembling goods) to an off-site team an ocean away and with whom you have no physical interaction or quality control mechanism. While you may have the highest trust that everyone is doing what they're supposed to, the bride whose flowers aren't delivered on time or the client who receives 500 logo key chains with the company name misspelled isn't going to mad at your helpers; they're going to be mad at you for allowing that mistake to happen in the first place.

*****

PAGING ALEX KEATON

Jeanette Chasworth (ASID) aka "The Color Whisperer" is a designer, author and speaker who loves to educate people about the power of color and design in their lives.

To say I'm passionate about the field of interior design is an understatement. Although I originally started out in marketing and publishing, I realized that it just wasn't where my heart was. With interior design, however, I fell hook, line and sinker and it has been my life ever since. I've had my own company for about ten years now and, as a sole proprietor, it's pretty much Me, Myself and I.

Until it comes to interns.

I've used interns for lots of different reasons. Mainly, though, it's for addressing all of the technical stuff I don't know how to do or for marketing activities that I just don't have the time for. Since I'm not as computer-savvy as they are, having that outside help is so nice!

I've also had design interns and use them to help do drafting and, thus, hone their skills. Because many of the projects are so in-depth, of course, I can only give them pieces I feel they can handle with their particular level of education and attention to detail.

One of the interns even helped me with my book, *What's Color Got To Do With It?* As a new author, I was struggling with it, and when I crossed paths at an American Society of Interior Designers (ASID) meeting with a student who had just produced a book she made from a computer program, my immediate thought was, "I need an intern!" I subsequently hired the first of two talented interns who helped me format everything together and finish it. They both knew stuff that I didn't know and they knew stuff that I wouldn't have thought of doing just because this is more their world, this is what they're being taught in school and I wasn't. So, those were good experiences. When an internship works out well, the intern comes away with something for his/her portfolio that could lead to a full-time job.

On the flip side have been not-so-great experiences.

You know, I think sometimes they just kind of get overwhelmed and they don't really realize what it is. I usually pay my interns - not very much - but it's about ten bucks an hour. One of my new interns realized I was charging $80 an hour to clients and exclaimed, "Oh my gosh, that's just a lot of money." Well, okay yes it is but it's not like I get paid 40 hours a week $80 an hour, you know? And even if I wanted to, I would be going crazy if I was billing out 40 hours a week.

So I gave her some paint samples that needed to be sorted and it took her an hour and a half. And I'm thinking, "No, no, no, no, no." Because she saw that $80 an hour, she was thinking, "Oh wow, Jeanette has got tons of money." I don't care how thorough you are, counting 1 to 150 does *not* take an hour and a half. When I realized why she did what she did and how she was approaching the task I'd given her, I saw it as a chance to educate her about the real world. "Look," I said, "there's billable time and there's not billable time." I gave her another chance and explained to her what being an entrepreneur really means. Unfortunately, this didn't sink in. She continued to give me overly inflated bills and we were done.

In my line of work, I get a lot of interns from the areas of fashion, computer design, and merchandising. There's a lot of foreign students, too, and they usually don't have cars. I recall one of them who asked me if I would pick her up from the train station which is ten minutes away. She sent me a bunch of emails and kept saying, "I really want to work with you, I really want to work with you." And, I said, "Ok, I'll give you a chance." I did it for a couple of weeks because I thought, "Well she really wants it and she really can help me with my various projects." Her work, however, was not high level. The trip to pick her up was more of a time suck than she helped while she was here, so that didn't go on very long.

Letting someone go, of course, is never a pleasant thing to do. To be honest, I've taken the easy way out sometimes and said, "I don't have anything for you to do" or I just didn't call them again. That is the joy of that type of situation, just saying "Well there's no work that I need." In cases where the student is an as-needed intern versus a semester intern, I just don't call them back. The interns who are logging hours seem to be much more dedicated and there are less problems.

On the positive side, hiring the interns to do the book was a smart decision. It was a skill I didn't have so I could give them ideas and they could just run with it. I can go over a project and say, "I like this, I like that, let's change this, let's change that," so the part that I can do we talk about. Obviously there's more supervision and monitoring involved in drafting because it's going to reflect on my business. I have certain ways I want things done and it has always helped that my interns weren't clean slates or novices. I've also had some where I put them to drafting and they could just do it so efficiently and effortlessly that they didn't need me constantly looking over their shoulders.

If you're going to hire interns, part of it is making sure from the outset that the skill is there. You have to ask yourself, "What skills do they have and how do I get the most out of them?" This last year I got a marketing intern from the local college and he built up my SEO. He just went and ran with it; I paid him ten bucks an hour and I'm now number one in Google. Since the SEO stuff was something I don't want to do myself or even want to know *how* to do, it's been very good for me.

Passion for one's craft also goes a very long way with me. If they're really passionate and they're really proficient, they're going to be someone I want to work with. I pay attention to their interview answers to see if they have what I'm looking for and what level of energy they bring to whatever I hire them to do for me. Getting back to my SEO guy, remember Alex Keaton from "Family Ties"? I'm like, "I'm sitting across from Alex Keaton, he's going to make me money and he's going to do this, and I don't have to worry." I knew in the first ten minutes this guy wants to be the head of X corporation by the time he's 30 and he's... ok, let's go!

You listen to what are they saying. You look at how they're presenting themselves. Do they show up on time? Are they dressed appropriately? Sometimes they'll ask me, "Do I need to dress up?" And I'll say, "Neh, you can wear jeans," but the fact they asked me shows that they would. I do a lot of student functions with ASID so sometimes I meet potential interns that way and am able to see them in a different situation before I even hire them. The questions they're asking, that tells me a lot. I also observe how they're reacting to other people around them because this is a very people-oriented business; if they're just kind of aloof and in the background, that's not somebody I want working for me. They need to be more present and involved in the task at hand.

When I hire an intern, it's usually for about two hours a week and it's for a semester. It depends on their schedule, too. With some internships you have to sign off on the hours and so those interns are more likely to show up. If you have one where you're *not* having to sign off on their hours, you'll hear, "Well I can't come this week." If you start getting that, then we're done anyway. I understand that other things are more important but they've made this commitment and I expect them to honor it. A really good intern is worth their weight in gold. A really bad intern is worth their weight in – well, you get the picture.

There are a lot of the design firms that use interns every semester. They might even get two interns every semester. It is a great opportunity for them to learn. Even though they often end up doing a lot of uninteresting tasks, like sorting samples. If they watch and learn, they will grow and may even get to stay on after the internship is over.

I've also observed that kids today have such a sense of entitlement that we can't even relate to because it just wasn't there for us. They seem to want everything to be convenient for them. With us, we would never have dreamed of asking an employer to drive us to and from work. We would have said, "I'll bring a bike, I'll walk, I'll find a bus schedule..."

They also don't like the phone; they just want to text all the time. A general complaint I hear from my peers about the interns - and even employees - is they don't want to talk on the phone. They just email or they text. And this business is very personal; you *have* to talk on the phone!

And don't even get me started on dress codes! Most of them don't have a clue how to dress properly.

When my interns are about to graduate, I always say, "Look, this is what you have to offer. You have technological skills that are way above and beyond previous generations. We don't want to learn those things ourselves and, more importantly, we don't have the time. We'd rather hire you to do it." And I say, "When you go into an interview, this is what you can do for us, and that's what you want to go in with, not what can we do for you. You have to look at it as, what can you do for us, what are your assets that you bring to the table?"

I also encourage them to ask questions. I don't ever want them to sit there starting at the computer for twenty minutes because they didn't understand something. No. There's no dumb question. I would much rather an intern - or anyone else - ask me a question than feel dumb or not be able to accomplish something because they didn't ask.

Having an intern can be a wonderful experience or a difficult one. Treat your intern as a new hire and make sure that they have skills that complement your needs and vice versa and you will have a good experience. This is a teaching situation and should be treated as such as well. It is a chance for you both to benefit. Be clear as to expectations, and everyone wins. You get the help you need and they get experience and knowledge.

*****

THE DELEGATION OF WORK

Leanne Hoagland-Smith has 30 years of practical business experience. She coaches, speaks and writes to quickly multiply results for people and businesses.

Going it alone is difficult for the solo entrepreneur. Taking care of everything from bookkeeping to marketing to selling to compliance to other necessary business operations every day leave many single office/home office (SOHO) business owners overwhelmed if not exhausted.

Isn't it rather ironic these dedicated entrepreneurs will reach out to accountants and even lawyers, but are hesitant to hire a:

- Web person to create their website or post updates.
- Social media to keep them noticed in the various social media streams.
- Marketing firm for their promotional products.
- Virtual assistant for daily operations.
- Independent sales representative to increase sales.

The question is why this hesitancy? In most instances, there are some available funds. If money is not the barrier, then what is keeping these overworked business professionals from moving forward and growing their businesses through delegation?

From my experience in working with solo-entrepreneurs, high income salespeople and small business owners, there are five shadow abilities behind successful delegation:

- The ability to let go.
- The ability to efficiently plan.
- The ability to develop a process.
- The ability to lead one's self first.
- The ability to effectively delegate.

Ability to Let Go

In the book, *The E-Myth*, the author Michael E. Gerber discusses this concept of too much working IN the business and not enough working ON the business. To work ON the business requires letting go of those daily business activities.

Letting go must happen first. This is a significant barrier for the SOHO because no one else knows his or her business like the SOHO. With time being a premium, these solo entrepreneurs rationalize it will take too much time to hire, to delegate others to do this work. And then who has the time to manage all these additional people and responsibilities is another frequent thought.

Not letting go is a mindset of scarcity and not one of abundance. Until this mindset changes, delegating any pressing business operations will ultimately fail. That failure will only reaffirm to the SOHO, he or she must do everything.

Ability to Effectively Plan

Planning is a critical skill set for anyone in any leadership role. General and President Dwight Eisenhower said "Plans are worthless; planning is everything."

Unfortunately, in today's business world, there are far too many "Captain Wing Its" and not enough "Captain Focus Its." The Captain Wing Its of the business world continually "spray their actions all over the place and then pray something will stick." Failure for business actions to stick in many instances is because these folks do not have the knowledge, skills, attitudes or habits for certain business operations. Again, they rationalize they do not have the time and in some instances the money to delegate these functions to others.

Effective planning (meaning doing the right thing) requires quiet time to think and returns to the first barrier of letting go. To work ON the business is very difficult when one is up to his or her arse in alligators to remember the initial objective was to drain the swamp as the expression goes. This is when a self-leadership comes into the picture. If one cannot lead one's self; how can he or she lead through delegation and management of others?

Additionally effective planning requires critical thinking skills. And again the barrier of letting go resurfaces. How can one think critically, objectively when his or her To Do list is higher than the Empire State Building?

The Ability to Develop a Process

Knowing when to say Uncle is not enough. Sure you can be up to your arse in alligators, but until you have a process to kill the alligators you may be eaten alive.

Seeking outside resources is necessary, but finding the right resources is critical. This is where your business to business network can support you.

To develop a process probably starts with two conversations, one with your accountant and a second one with your attorney. These two individuals can help you establish some key benchmarks to determine when you can move forward by hiring other vendors.

Next step is doing your research including:

- Asking within your business to business network for referrals.
- Reaching out to the Better Business Bureau.
- Googling the proposed vendor.

Yes this takes time as does interviewing prospective vendors. What unfortunately happens is many solo entrepreneurs in a rush to have a website, hire a social media or marketing person or any other vendor make a reactive decision that is unfortunately very costly (think profit draining). By documenting your process you ultimately save far more time than you initially invest not to mention dollars.

The Ability to Lead One's Self

Much is written about leadership and leading others. Far less is written about leading one's self or what I call self-leadership.

Leading one's self goes beyond the plethora of self-improvement books or workshops. This is truly a disciplined behavior that recognizes each individual has unique talents as well as limitations. By knowing those talents and those limiting skills provides the opportunity for clarity.

Here is where having clarity around one's purpose, vision, values and current mission come into the picture. Additionally, consistently employing a proven goal setting and goal achievement process is critical.

To lead one's self may require finding a mentor or hiring a small business coach or consultant. Such action also demands scheduling time and once again we return to the previous challenges of letting go, efficiently planning and developing a process.

The Ability to Successfully Delegate

Delegation is a skill set, a well honed skill set. Good to great management of one's self in managing others is the end result of effective delegation. This is the end result of realizing the first four abilities.

- If one cannot let go, one cannot successfully delegate
- If one cannot effectively plan, one cannot successfully delegate
- If one cannot develop a process, one cannot successfully delegate
- If one cannot lead himself or herself, one cannot successfully delegate

Successful delegation is not one simple act, one stroke of the pen. No, far more is required to achieve the results of delegating and, therefore, managing others. When these first four barriers are ignored, the result is usually chaos for the solo entrepreneur.

When solo entrepreneurs develop these five abilities and grow their businesses, again from my experience, they will indeed be ahead of the flow. Now is the time to determine which barrier or barriers you as that SOHO, budding small business owner must address so you can successfully delegate many of those "To Do" items that are restricting your business growth.

*****

MANAGING YOUR "AWAY TEAM"

Wendy Anderson is the owner of WOW! Event Productions in Pasadena, California and frequently orchestrates events that attract tens of thousands attendees.

When was the last time you went to an artisan faire? A job expo? A booksellers' convention? A classic car show? Chances are that by the time the gates opened to admit the first wave of attendees, the coffee cantinas were already dispensing refreshments, the speakers and presenters were amicably chatting with one another on the dais, the vendors' wares were neatly displayed for purchase, and the map to feature attractions was not only accurate but also a breeze to navigate.

If you've never put together a large-scale production with a lot of moving parts and complex timeframes, you might assume that the person in charge simply told all of the participants, "Be at such-and-such address at 8 a.m. with whatever stuff you're bringing" and everyone would automatically know what to do and where to set up when they got there. In a perfect world, that would sure make an event planner's life like mine much easier! In reality, though, that approach would be like trying to herd cats. The result? Chaos!

Working with volunteers, subcontractors and vendors on specific, short-term projects is a lot different from managing employees that you see on a regular basis. The latter has had time to get to know your leadership style and expectations just as you've had time to observe their strengths and weaknesses, especially under pressure. When you're working with what I call the "away team," however, you're trusting strangers to do exactly what you want in the absence of close supervision.

The years of operating as a sole proprietor have taught me that the key to successfully managing an away team of virtually any size has several layers. Here are some of the lessons I'd like to share.

First of all, never forget that whatever you're doing is always for your client; no matter what problems big or small a subcontractor may create, the buck stops with you. Regardless of the number of helping hands you assemble for your temporary team, you're the one the client is going to hold accountable for everything that occurs (including any publicity that reflects badly on your client's image).

Secondly, it's essential to establish your leadership right from the start. Oftentimes you might hire a subcontractor that has more experience or knowledge about a particular aspect of the project than you do. It's obviously important to recognize their strength on the team but to make sure in the eyes of the whole team and your client that you are the leader. All key decisions pertaining to your team members and your client must remain firmly in your hands.

Never be intimidated or jealous of the skills, knowledge and abilities of any subcontractor you hire. Promote their strong points in the project. Hold them out as the expert in the area if indeed they are. Their strength will only make your work on this project more golden! If they come up with great ideas, acknowledge and embrace that contribution; don't turn around and make it 'your idea'. Creating a strong team whether it is one subcontractor or a team of subs isn't easy. Embrace everyone's strength and you'll help to create a dynamite corps.

Sometimes you may already know the person who's going to be providing contract services, maybe not in a current working relationship but, rather, as a business or personal association. Don't assume, however, that just because you may know them in that context you'll be able to work with them in your particular business situation. I strongly suggest that you interview them just as you would any other subcontractor. Ask questions on what they would do given certain scenarios so you have a better idea how you communicate with them or how they may interact with the rest of the team as well as your client.

No matter the depth of the friendship, business is business and should be maintained and handled in that manner. You never know until you work with someone what their style is and if, in fact, it's even compatible with your own way of doing business and completing tasks. If it's simply not working out to your expectations, hard decisions may have to be made in order to preserve the friendship as well as keep the project from being jeopardized or compromised.

Always create a working contract with your participants before the project gets underway. If they'll have access to materials you have created, for instance, make sure that this is specified in the contract and that they don't have the right to copy or utilize any materials or contacts lists developed by your company. Identify delegated assignments, timelines and payment schedules so everyone know what is expected of them, when it needs to be completed, and how they will be reimbursed.

It's also critical not only to have a clear means of communication but also to articulate how the communication will be between you and your away team. My own style is very inclusive and often labeled as 'controlling' but, again, it's my client and any 'fall in the crack' or miscommunication falls on me and not my subcontractors. If, for example, you're a strong communicator via email and your sub is not, this may create issues, especially if it's a team you're leading and you're not getting timely responses from them. Establish the team's means to communicate and make sure to maintain it. If it's not being adhered to, address it directly with them and as soon as possible. Oftentimes it's more practical that communication be via email to the whole group versus individual phone calls and one-on-one meetings. This way everyone is not only in the loop but there is documentation as well of instructions, comments, ideas, and resolutions.

One of the hardest areas of any company is personnel. As a sole proprietor hiring subcontractors and negotiating with vendors, treat them with respect just as you would if they were your employees. Make them a part of your project so they embrace it and want to make sure everything comes off perfectly. If there are instances, however, where one of them isn't living up to expectations or is causing work to fall behind schedule, stop and think about it first. Then have a heart-to-heart conversation. Don't immediately come down on the person. There may be some serious personal issues happening in their life. Usually when you handle a difficult subject calmly and straightforward, it's better received and resolved.

There's no question that a dynamite team of subcontractors will help elevate your professionalism as a sole proprietor in the eyes of your clients as well as everyone they subsequently talk to about your work. It all starts with exercising strong leadership skills, respecting what each member of your proposed team has to offer, and utilizing a framework of communication guidelines that keeps everyone on the same page.

THE FRUGAL MARKETER

In order to make money, you'll likely have to spend money. At the same time, it's not good business to spend money you don't actually have, especially if you're spending it on all the wrong things. Unless you're launching your sole proprietorship with the help of a trust fund, a wealthy spouse or a winning lottery ticket, you're watching your budget with an eagle eye and trying to decide how to allocate limited resources.

There's a big difference between doing things on the cheap and doing things economically. Many an entrepreneur, for instance, has gone the selfie route rather than hire a photographer to take a professional headshot. Whether these casual candids are shot at arm's length, into a mirror, or with a self-timing camera on a shelf or tripod, they have become the latest excuse for people who think professional photographers charge too much. "Maybe down the road when I'm more established," a debut author told me, "but for right now I can't afford those kind of fees."

Frankly, she can't afford *not* to make that investment. Consider the impression you want to leave with your prospective customers. A bad DIY job is worse than doing nothing at all because it communicates two things: (1) you're not successful enough to afford a high quality shoot and (2) you're arrogant enough to believe that you know more about taking pictures of yourself than a trained studio professional. That you didn't take the time or spend the money to (literally) put your best face forward runs the additional risk of advancing the one message you never intended; specifically, maybe that same lack of effort was put toward the very product or service you're trying to sell.

I've also seen no shortage of entrepreneurs who try to design their own marketing materials (i.e., business cards, brochures, fliers, print ads). They've never taken a class in graphic design…and it shows. I recall a script consultant who asked my opinion of her tri-fold brochure which was not only photocopied on 20# goldenrod bond but had also gone through the machine on the slant. Knowing what she was charging for her consulting services, I asked why she wasn't investing more money in upgrading her handout materials. Her response: "Oh everyone just leaves them on their chairs anyway so why should I?" Hmmm.

At the other end of the equation are people who spend more on appearances rather than substance. One such case was an aspiring young filmmaker from Hong Kong who believed that the first thing he needed to do to be taken seriously was lease an office, furniture and equipment and hire a receptionist. He had yet to launch a website, decide what kind of films he wanted to produce, create a marketing plan, or network with any kindred spirits in the movie industry. A friend of his, he said, was also starting a film company but went to Starbucks everyday with his laptop and cell phone because a brick and mortar office wasn't in his start-up budget. Guess which one is still in business?

*****

THE LONE WOLF

Mindy Littman Holland was sole proprietor of Littman & Associates, a marketing communications and public relations business, for 20+ years.

Nineteen eighty-seven was a pivotal year for me. I left two corporations, miscarried a four-month pregnancy, filed for divorce, met my future husband and started my own marketing and public relations business, all at the same time. When associates learned that I was preparing to leave the inner ranks of the corporate world, several approached me to form partnerships and/or agencies. I politely but firmly declined because, for the first time in my working life, I was going to have a little flexibility and I only wanted one person to answer to – me. I didn't want to commute to an office at the crack of dawn in Atlanta's horrendous rush-hour traffic; I didn't want to be responsible for direct employees; I didn't want anyone to assist me with decision-making. I wanted to be a lone wolf.

That's not to say I shunned collaborative efforts at client sites. Just the opposite. In fact, I often became an integral member of the in-house marketing team, if there was one. Sometimes I served as an entire marketing department for smaller companies. Once they were ready to hire in-house, full-time employees, I assisted with the interviews, hiring and training and I continued to serve as outside counsel as long as they needed me.

I like being an outsider. Outsiders get more respect. One of my clients once said to me, "Why is it when I present a plan I'm an idiot and when you present the same plan you're a genius?" "It's because I'm an outsider," I told him. I don't know why but when a company pays an outsider for advice, they seem to have more confidence in the outcome. I always had numerous requests to do contract work, even when I was working 80 hours a week for "the man." So, when I decided to go out on my own, I had an immediate client base. I never took on more than I could service fully (usually four clients at a time). And I only took on clients that weren't going to be a colossal pain in my ass.

If an organization wanted me to do something I had never done before, I would advise them of my inexperience and say, "If you are willing to give me the opportunity to do this job for you, I will give it my very best shot. If you don't like the result, you don't have to pay me." I learned what I was especially good at (anything that involved oral or written communications) and what I enjoyed doing most (ditto) and what I could do without (don't ask!) – and I always got paid.

Because life was so complicated when I started my own business, I wanted to keep things as simple as possible. As I mentioned previously, that meant no legal partnerships, limited or otherwise. It also meant no office outside of my own home (except for the offices my clients provided me at their sites). And it meant no direct reports. I did hire subcontractors on an ad hoc basis. I gave my clients the option of paying the subs directly or having me bill for their services with a 25% markup. I tried not to be out of pocket because some of the printing jobs were very pricey and, while my payment terms were typically Net 30, some companies didn't pay that quickly. I did whatever I could to keep my overhead to a minimum.

I started (and ended) my business with a PC and a Mac, a printer, a fax machine, a telephone, an old-fashioned typewriter and access to the Internet. That was all I needed to conduct business with clients all over the world. And I worked out of my finished basement. I slid down a banister and I was on the job! Many of my clients were out-of-towners, but if a local client wanted a face-to-face meeting, I tried to set it up for between 10 a.m. and 3 p.m. so I wouldn't waste a monstrous amount of time mired in traffic. Sometimes, I was still working with overseas clients at 2 a.m. But if I wanted to run around the neighborhood for an hour at 9 a.m. or 9 p.m. or work in my jammies, I just did it. Ah, flexibility!

There might have been tax advantages to forming a subchapter S corporation, but I opted to be a sole proprietor. I secured an Employer ID Number, opened two Keogh accounts, which are tax-deferred pension plans for self-employed individuals, and religiously filed the requisite 5500 forms (which I hated like poison – thank God my father was a CPA). I paid quarterly estimated taxes, took a home office deduction (until three years before I knew I was going to sell my house. Sometimes there are benefits to NOT claiming a portion of your house as office space. Speak to your CPA – the rules may have changed over the past several years). I kept very careful track of out-of-pocket expenses and business-related miles. And, if I were traveling on behalf of a client, I let them make and pay for the arrangements.

After more than 20 years, I moved to Santa Fe, NM where people offered me plenty of work if I were willing to work for free. So I shut down the business, turned the Keoghs into traditional IRAs and became a published author, photographer, artist, blogger and dancing fool. I still have great relationships with many of my former clients. They are now my friends. Our entrepreneurial spirits have taken us elsewhere. We hang out together. We embrace when we meet. We don't earn as much as we used to but life is richer. And simpler.

*****

DOLLARS AND SENSE

Corine La Font is a self-publishing, online marketing and virtual events consultant and specialist based in Kingston, Jamaica.

Unless you knew from a very young age that you wanted to be your own boss and started saving up towards that goal, then it's time to get innovative and think out-of-the-box fast in order to achieve the objectives you have set for yourself. Many budding entrepreneurs may not have an idea as to what their focus may be yet and that's okay. Keep searching and observing others who run successful businesses. When you've found that one thing that makes you wake up in the morning and not want to go to sleep at nights, write it down and start planning! You see, finding a business or idea that you're passionate about makes marketing it less of a chore because you love what you do.

On the other hand, there is the belief that once you're making money, it doesn't matter whether you love it or not. I leave that decision to you. Either way, you want to start off with little to no expenses and the one line-item that takes up a significant part of the budget is marketing. Without marketing, no one will know you exist and have something really amazing to offer. Marketing is also an activity that never stops. It follows the 80/20 rule – 80% marketing with 20% work in the business.

Marketing however, is not as hard as it seems. The thing is that if you don't have the extra cash to invest, it only means you have to put in the time instead – sweat equity.
Let's look at some very inexpensive ways you can apply today to get your sole proprietor business off the ground and into the minds and hearts of your target audience.

1. Social Media Marketing: It is free to set up social media accounts on Facebook, Twitter, Linkedin and Google+. There are social media management software programs such as Hootsuite and tweetdeck to manage those accounts. The free versions come with limited features but it is a great start to effectively use your time when scheduling posts, tweets and updates to your network.
2. Contests: Everyone loves to participate in contests to win something. You may, for example, want to offer a free coaching session to the winner. These contests can also be integrated on your social networks and as part of the rules to enter, contestants can be required to share, like or tweet a message to others to be rewarded with a certain number of entries. Using this approach with rafflecopter.com has the added benefit of leveraging your network to broaden your reach in the market.
3. Opt-ins and newsletters: While contests certainly help to build your list, it only happens on occasions. To create sustainability, another great way to build your list is to

give away something of perceived value for free. Let's say you wrote an ebook. You can give away a chapter of that book or newsletter in return for the names and email addresses of prospects. The power is in the list, for it is this list that will enable you build a relationship and loyalty which, over time, creates opportunities to sell, cross-sell or even up-sell your products and services. A useful resource such as Mailchimp allows you to send out 12,000 mails to your list for free. Higher than this amount requires a small fee. Mailchimp is such a flexible application that they even offer a pay-per-use fee that is more than reasonable even for those of you who are on a minimal budget.

4. Blog, Virtual Blog Tour, Guest Blogging: Blogs are free and easy to set up but they run the risk of being taken down or removed if it is found that you are selling on the site. Recommended sites are Wordpress or Blogger. Who says you can't tour the world and promote yourself and your business? Using a self-hosted blog site, reach out to others who have blogs attracting a similar but larger audience that you can approach to request that they be a host on your tour. Of course, you will have to negotiate what they will get in return. Always try to create a win-win situation for all involved. Don't want to spend the time doing a full 15 or 30 day virtual blog tour? No problem. Determine if your hosts would be willing to have you write a guest blog for them on occasions to be posted on their site. Everyone is always looking for great content which they themselves don't have time to write. Another win-win situation I say and you both leverage each other's visitors and prospects.

5. Get on radio or have your own radio show: Online radio is one of your best bets if you are having a challenge with getting traditional radio interviews. Submit your information to radioguestlist.com and wait for the radio hosts to contact you. Can't wait for that? Take some initiative and reach out to the hosts in the category of your choice on blogtalkradio.com. It worked for me, so it will work for you, too. Wait! Why not own your own radio show? Yes, Blogtalkradio offers that option as well! Interview guests that you can learn from and teach your audience, build your following and listeners, and actively seek to repurpose all that great

content you would have archived into products that you can make money from.

6. Build your sales team: If you have some extra funds, why not create your own digital products such as ebooks, training courses or coaching on your own branded affiliate platform? Check out Wordpress' affiliate platform. Easy to set up, install and configure for a one-time fee of $49.95. With this approach, you will have your very own sales team of affiliates and pay by commission.

While almost all the above can be implemented for free one thing you need to remember is that the level of your investment - time and/or money - is directly proportionate to your results. On the other hand, there are unexpected results which can be a welcome surprise. As an author-preneur, solo-preneur or entrepreneur, your results may vary based on the business you are in, customer service delivery, pricing, demand and much more. In marketing, like with Forrest Gump, you never know what you're gonna get, so enjoy the journey and relish in the destination!

*****

LET'S GIVE THEM SOMETHING TO TALK ABOUT

Garrett Mehrguth, is President and CEO of Directive Consulting and specializes in digital consulting, developing, and marketing for small to medium size businesses.

Marketing is tough when you're a sole proprietor. Harnessing the power of word-of-mouth is even tougher. If you can empower your customer then you can drive more sales to your business by marketing through the simple art of conversation. The question is how do you get your customers to start talking about your business?

Customers=Friends

Distancing yourself from your clients is a giant no-no. Think about it: would you rather tell someone else about your friend or a random person? By focusing on relationships with your customers and demonstrating that you care about them at a level deeper than business is powerful. Here are a few ways to do this:

- Get their address…people love getting stuff in the mail
- Call them on their birthday
- Write them a note…you have their address, right?
- Ask about their family
- Buy their animal a toy…animals can talk, too, right?

All these ideas fit on a shoestring budget. You don't have to do all of them at once, either. Be calculated and unique for each of your friends. Friends know what other friends like.

Make the Boring Extraordinary

Coffee isn't that exciting…but it can be. Sure, we love it and it has moved into the realm of inelasticity, but it's just a bean, right? Wrong. What about the process? Imagine if you are a coffee shop owner and you highlighted the process of how you attained your coffee? In case you didn't know how coffee goes from the field to your cup, the normal process is as follows:

1. Plant
2. Harvest
3. Process
4. Dry
5. Mill
6. Export
7. Taste
8. Roast
9. Grind
10. Brew

However, what if you could highlight one of these aspects that make your particular coffee extraordinary? You see, extraordinary things get talked about far more often than the un-extraordinary. Do a little social experiment and look at your social media feeds. Chances are you will find a friend of yours sharing something extraordinary. Ever seen a photo of a lamp on your Instagram feed?

Anyways, back to the coffee. While almost all of us

brew our coffee hot, there is another way. An extraordinary way. What if you brewed your coffee *cold*? The normal ritual from the coffee snobs to the "I like it black's" is the same. You wake up. Drudge to the kitchen and make your coffee with the click of a switch and your coffee is brewed...hot.

Cold brewed coffee is as different as the name suggests. With cold brewed coffee, you avoid the downfall of hot brewed coffee...the acid. According to the National Heartburn Alliance, of the estimated 54 million Americans who suffer heartburn, 75% say beverages such as coffee can cause it.

By stressing the inherent remarkability of cold brewed coffee you harness the power of marketing through word-of-mouth. By simply changing your brewing technique and highlighting its uniqueness, you have suddenly differentiated yourself in an extraordinary way. Your own product or service can and is just as remarkable; you just need to delve deeper into understanding what exactly make you, your product, or your service remarkable.

Let's Get Creative

Grasping the internal remarkability of your product or service is no easy task. Below are a few things you can do to get the creative juices flowing:

- Break down the value chain process of your product or service. Look for differentiators.
- Think about what would happen if your product or service disappeared. Why would the world not be the same?
- List 5 reasons for why you came into business in the first place

Getting Your Friends to Talk About You

Have you ever gone to a nice restaurant and experienced top class service and world-class food? If you are anything like me, you rave about it. You can't help but invite your friends to your newfound gem.

Word-of-mouth spreads like wildfire the moment you secure your brand's first advocate. How do you earn that first advocate? The simple answer is to treat everyone as a friend and exceed his or her expectations. Easier said than done. Oftentimes, even our closest friends have wildly unrealistic expectations. You can try to control and frame these expectations; however, you only have so much control of expectations. Nevertheless, treating someone else as you would like to be treated is entirely within your control. By servicing your friends in an extraordinary manner, you have lit the wick.

Remember that other people love being remarkable just as much as you do. Let them be remarkable by telling their friends about your extraordinary product or service.

*****

PICTURES WORTH A THOUSAND WORDS...BUT NOT COSTING THOUSANDS OF DOLLARS

Minnesota author Jan Dunlap is an accomplished speaker, insightful writer and wickedly humorous guest blogger for a wide range of writing, marketing and spirituality websites.

"It's all about the image!" may be a timeworn piece of advice for celebrities, but in today's social networking milieu, those words have taken on a twist for anyone who wants to stay in front of the public: visual images drive engagement of audience. Studies show, for example, that 1) you'll get a 37% increase in engagement when you include photos with a Facebook post, 2) Pinterest usage grew more than one thousand percent in its first year, and 3) Instagram photos score more than a billion likes per day.

So how can you argue against using lots of photos and images in social marketing for your solo business? Not to mention that every other kind of visual marketing you do, ranging from letterheads/logos to brochures to even old-fashioned flyers and print ads, depend on effective visual content. The simple fact is that you have to work with images since that's how your potential customers form their first, all-important impression of you.

If you're like me – camera-confused and design-disabled – you may be well into panic mode at this point. But fear not, my similarly artistically-challenged friends! There's a plenitude of image resources that you can access and master to launch your social networking marketing

146

game. They may not rank with the work of Andy Warhol or Monet, but they're easy and free, and they're your tickets to spurring audience engagement, which is your first step of the marketing process. Here are a few of my favorites:

1. Microsoft Word Clip-art. Really. I find great photos right on my own software. Go to Word, hit insert , then clip-art, and start browsing for the ones that catch your eye or nail your subject. You can easily crop photos to fit your needs. Remember, it doesn't have to be mind-blowing art; it just needs to catch your reader's eye long enough for them to react, and (hopefully) read the accompanying post. I've had terrific shares using clip-art photos and even been asked where I got the great shots from!

2. PowerPoint. I routinely use this to create promotional materials and then save the images as jpegs to use online. I pick a slide layout, insert photos or other images/text, and I'm done. It's my go-to choice for producing new Facebook banners or any tiled visuals to freshen up posts or spotlight upcoming events. It's also extremely useful for creating posters and flyers which you can then produce right on your own printer. An added benefit is that these layouts are graphically effective because they balance text and images (which we'll revisit below).

3. PicMonkey. I was totally intimidated by this site until I actually tried to produce an image on it. It was a snap! And to make it even more of a no-brainer, I used photos from Word's clip-art collection to begin the process. If you use one of the free image sites, like everystockphoto.com or FreeDigitalPhotos.net, you can expand your image-generating capacity even more. Just be sure to check for licenses and give credit when it's required. Simply search for "Free Images" and you'll find a list of sites you can tap into.

4. Pixabay. Here's my newest favorite site for finding exactly the photo you're looking for. With a collection of over 230,000 free photos, illustrations and graphics, you can find the perfect image and create your own postcard/poster-like posts (using PicMonkey to add the text) for maximum impact.

There are other image-producing sites you can explore, but since I want to keep focused on my business (and not the advertising tasks it requires), I rely on these four resources to give me the visual content I want with minimal investment of time and painful effort; the unexpected bonus is that when it's easy to create images for online networking, you'll be more apt to do it more frequently, which is a key to social networking promotion success. And by changing it up with different images and text, you keep your audience engaged as you tell the story of your business...one nugget at a time.

That leads to the other key of marketing success: give your audience just enough information in your advertising to keep them intrigued enough to take the next step – whether it's an online trip to your website or a phone call/email to your business. Sales are built on trust, and you need to assure your customers every step of the advertising way that their satisfaction is your prime objective. Information overload scares customers, so court them one step at a time with concise, easily consumed, advertising messages. One of the biggest mistakes many sole proprietors make in their advertising is succumbing to the temptation to spill ALL their beans at once to their audience.

Like I said, BIG mistake. It's bad enough when you see a print ad (or PowerPoint presentation) that is so filled with text you give up after reading the first ten words, but in the online world, you have between 3 and 5 seconds to make a first impression. And what speaks faster, and much more effectively than a block of text?

You guessed it: Images.

Yes, you need a bit of text; at a minimum, include a link to your website, or a memorable tagline about your product (preferably both!). But if you really want to make the most of that 3 to 5-second window, go for an image that fires the emotions, and then add a bit of persuasive copy that convinces your potential customer to take that next step in the sales transaction (marketing pros call it the CTA – Call To Action).

Ready? Set? Go forth...with image!

CRACKING THE MEDIA CODE

Spring is the time of year when we roll up our sleeves, take stock of our accumulated clutter, and commit to the task of getting better organized. Obviously this would be a less daunting exercise if we simply kept our house in order *all the time* and ready to entertain guests at a moment's notice.

Could your company's media plan pass the same test of readiness?

No matter what passion you've chosen to pursue as a business owner, getting – and staying – prepared for a call from the media is job #1.

Several years ago I made an offer to a solopreneur who also happened to be a personal friend. In these tough economic times, I knew she was struggling to stay afloat and, further, she couldn't afford to hire a PR firm to help generate a buzz. "Tell you what," I said, "if you can provide me with the answers to a few interview questions along with a great photograph to accompany the article, I can get the story out there within two weeks."

She was appreciative and effusive in her enthusiasm and promised she'd work on the questionnaire on her days off. Time passed. When I followed up to see what was accounting for the delay, she replied, "You know, I'm way too tired on my days off to spend them doing any work but maybe I can throw something together for you by the end of next month."

Throw something together?

This prompts three disturbing questions. The first is whether she felt it wasn't necessary to treat the offer seriously because it was coming from someone she knew, someone who could say, "Oh, there, there. Really, it's all right. Take your time. And whenever you get back to me, I'll just drop everything else I'm doing." Secondly, was there some naiveté in play which led her to think that media opportunities come along like busses every ten minutes? If so, why are they not regularly making stops outside her front door? Thirdly – and perhaps the most alarming – how can anyone who has run their own business for more than 24 hours not have a press kit available in case someone requests it? There should be no mad scramble to assemble clips, get testimonials, compose snappy quotes, or grab a digital camera. Sadly, this slapdash mindset isn't uncommon, especially with sole proprietors who either never expect to garner media attention or don't understand that press deadlines aren't fluid.

For future reference, they'd be wise to take a page from HR specialists who recommend keeping your resume up-to-date. Even if you're happy as a clam in your current job and have no plans to leave, a dream opportunity with a short window could suddenly present itself.

Such was my own experience back in the 70's when I ran into a friend I hadn't seen for a while. She was lunching with a colleague who let it drop she had a position to fill and was dreading the upcoming process of advertising it, then interviewing candidates. By the time she returned to her office, there was a fax waiting for her: my resume. Not only did I get the job but I also met my first husband, started an acting company, and was able to return to college. If being prepared can produce that magnitude of life-changing fortune, imagine what could happen to *your* business if you're prepared when media opportunities knock?

MEDIA READINESS

Cecelia Haddad's expertise lies in developing a long term vision and strategy for clients with inherent consideration of the bottom line.

It's important that you be media ready. But what does that mean? What it *doesn't* mean is only being ready with the answers to the questions that you want to be asked. What it does mean is that you are prepared and primed to be considered a leader in your field of expertise and able to provide both company information and value added information about your industry sector.

A sole proprietor can become media ready by getting professional training which would assist with the two key things you need to know before an interview:

Messaging – The ability to answer any question.

Development of a media Q&A – write down all the questions you think a journalist might ask you but not just the ones you want to be asked. Start with the questions you DON'T want to be asked and develop an answer for each. The answers should be short and sharp and no more than three sentences long.

Technique – What you need to master including those peculiar to television, print and radio.

Watch the news and current affairs programs – ABC's Four Corners and the like are great resources. Study the person being interviewed – did you believe what they said – why or why not? Words are only part of your story but if your expression is saying something else you have immediately lost credibility. Practice saying the answers to your questions out loud. Better still video this or ask a friend or colleague to watch you. They can point out things you may not be aware of, for example, scratching your nose when trying to think of an answer. It is those little things that can distract the audience from what you are saying.

Keep your options open with it comes to working with journalists – don't limit yourself. Determining which journalists to work with (and therefore which media) comes down to two things:

- Is your message relevant to that media?
- Do the media reach the audience that you are trying to target?

If you can answer yes to both those questions then you can work out who to target accordingly. From experience, some of the clients I work with require us to have several different media target lists depending on our message and audience. Having said that, it is always good practice to develop solid relationships with journalists remembering that it doesn't matter how good that relationship is, you still need a good story to get media coverage.

As a sole proprietor, you can reach the media by working out who your target audience is and then what they read, watch and listen to. Most PR professionals subscribe to media databases but these are expensive and you usually need to enter into a long term contract. Once you find the media you want to contact email is usually a good option or pick up the phone and be ready with your 30-second elevator pitch. A product or service push is really not going to cut it, so make sure your pitch is about what the media's audience is going to get out of the story. Writing good Op Ed (opinion) pieces can help establish leadership in your field and if you are entwined in social media, then blog posts, twitter feeds and LinkedIn posts are a great way to get noticed by journalists. Use these mediums to build your profile as an expert.

If you ever face a crisis, there is NEVER a time to use the words "NO COMMENT". A response such as this will certainly send a message to your audience but it won't be the one you want. It immediately implies guilt. Can't comment or won't comment? If you can't comment (for example if the situation is under legal investigation) you can say "I am unable to comment because this situation is under a legal investigation" and then something like "But I am working with the authorities to assist in their investigations" of course depending on what the situation is.

If you won't comment – then you shouldn't be a spokesperson in the first place. There are many ways to answer a question you don't want to answer – and frankly we get these types of questions in our everyday lives. As the spokesperson you must comment – you have just spent an enormous amount of your life establishing your reputation and expertise so now is not the time to back away and watch that all go down the drain. Here are some useful alternatives:

- "I think it would be clearer if I first explained...."
- "I don't have all the facts to be able to answer that question accurately but I can tell you that ..." (continue with your key message),
- "To answer that you must consider the following points..."
- "Your question points out a misconception we hear too often. The real issue here is ..."
- "Actually that relates to a more important concern..."

Here's an example how being prepared pays off after you and your business have been involved in a crisis:

I had a client a number of years ago entering into a partnership with another company. The other company had been involved in a crisis years before but it had all been sorted and they were back on track. I told my client he needed to be prepared to be asked a question about this partner's history. He thought it was so long ago it wouldn't matter but I told him 'mud sticks' and let's rehearse it anyway, it can't hurt right? Well, as I predicted, the journalist asked that exact question and my client was ready; he delivered his answer beautifully and the journalist moved on. No harm done, but it was an opportunity to put that issue to bed because even if the journalist hadn't asked, the audience may have been wondering. It pays to be prepared!

All interviews start with a 50/50 balance between you and the journalist. Taking control of an interview can be difficult, particularly if the journalist has a particular angle they would like to pursue. However whether you have instigated the interview or the journalist has approached you, the main thing to remember is why you are doing the interview. It could be to raise your profile as an expert in your field or to promote your particular product or service. Regardless of the intention, you will need to prepare for the interview with two or three strong key messages. Managing the interview involves being able to respond to most questions with your key messages regardless of the question. A good way to do this is to write down you key messages, then write them down again but rephrasing them. Don't over-rehearse but during the interview keep looking for ways to say what you really need your audience to hear.

To stay on track during a media interview remember why you are doing the interview and to keep trying to find opportunities to weave in your key messages. If you feel the interview is going off-track and you are asked something that isn't the direction you would like to head you can use what we call bridging techniques.

As a sole proprietor, you want to appear confident and this comes from preparation. Have you ever tried to do an exam without studying? It just doesn't work. Media interviews are the same. If you know your stuff, then all you have to do is focus on your technique: smiling when appropriate, maintaining your composure, listening carefully and answering thoughtfully. Practicing in front of a colleague or friend is helpful in picking up any nervous gestures for example, rubbing your chin, fidgeting with your hands. Some people don't even know they do them and quite often in my training when I play the film back they say, "Wow I didn't know I did that!" So these are the things to avoid doing during an interview.

First impressions are everything. Clothing should be both appropriate to your job and appropriate for the medium. If you are in a corporate / professional role you should dress accordingly. There are a few clothing tips I would give for television though – do not wear solid red, solid white or stripes (it plays havoc with the camera). In all cases, do not let your clothes overshadow what you have to say. So unless your career is as a clown I would keep it classy, simple and appropriate for your job.

If you're on the shy side, keep in mind that shyness can be mistaken for lack of confidence and can even lead to obvious physical signs such as blushing or sweating. In an interview situation, the audience (and the journalist) wants to be confident that you know what you are talking about so it is important to be able to overcome your shyness during an interview. Confidence can help. Make sure you know your subject matter extremely well. If someone asked you where you lived you could confidently answer that question. You need to project that confidence with your answers to interview questions.

Apart from knowing *what* to say, it is also *how* you say it. Use a confident tone in your voice that descends not rises (like a question), and where possible try to match the tone that the interviewer is using. Take a deep breath and pause before you answer, rather than stumbling and fumbling through a question.

Being media ready is of the utmost importance to a sole proprietor. Again, you'll want to get some type of media training; it will help with your messaging, technique, confidence and be a skill that you can take into other parts of your work such as presentations and new business pitches. Most importantly, remember that *nothing* is ever off the record.

*****

PERFECTING THE PRESS KIT

Lana McAra is an award-winning author of 20 titles with more than half a million books sold writing under the name Rosey Dow. She's an owner of Busy Bees Unlimited, LLC.

A press kit is a series of documents that are prepared to give to the media. It's more than one document – it can be anywhere from 3-6 different documents that are put into a kit. In the old days, they were printed out on glossy paper and put into folders and mail them out to various press, media people, such as magazines, newspapers, radio and TV. The media people would open the kits and then based on what they say, they would call for an interview.

Today's press kit is different. You can do all of the above by email, so very few people mail press kits any more, especially after the mailing scares some have experienced. Many people won't accept an envelope in the mail. So... it's all done by email or posted online on your website.

The press kit is structured in many ways because different people want different things. And depending on your industry or public relations agencies that are representing you or whatever, it can be done a lot of a different ways.

The components of a press kit are as follows:

Press release. You'll want to update your press release regularly to ensure it has the most up-to-date information about your product or service.

One-sheet. A one-sheet is like a one page ad. It has your picture, bio and other pertinent information. They can be printed up like a flyer, so it looks good.

An extended bio. This bio has more detail about you

and your business.

Interview questions. Not only can you include interview questions, but you can include speaking topics. The media will look over your speaking points and basically know what you'll be speaking about. You may consider including a signature speech.

List of influencers. These are people who can speak for you. For example, you may include a list of testimonials, references, reviews and more.

The press kit should be formatted; it should look good and be professionally created. You'll want to include your contact information on the bottom of each piece so the media knows how to contact you, include your phone number, email address and website.

Everyone in business, no matter if you're a CPA or plumber, needs a press kit. You are experts at what you do. The way to grow a business is to get exposure. Having a press kit would be such an in, such a boost, to getting started. Keep in mind that if you were to get an interview, people would get a chance to know you and what it is you do. You would get exposure and gain new clients and/or customers. Here's an example:

If you're in the skilled trades, let's say electrician or interior designer, there are shows out there about home design and remodeling. You would come in and talk as an expert about some new thing that's coming along in home remodeling. You may also be part of a panel of experts discussing a particular topic.

Keep in mind that there are radio shows on many topics from how to fix your car to how to garden. There's all type of media out there waiting to hear from you. But the trick is to position yourself as an expert who knows about your field, who can speak to it. Here's another example:

I met a man who had a power washing

company. This may seem like a simple, straightforward trade, but he took time to dictate a book to his wife. It was about a 50 page book on tips for power washing – do it yourself publishing. He self-published it and he next thing you know the press kit came along with that, and he started to get interviews. His business went from $50,000 a year to $250,000 a year because he was out there as an expert.

The average cost of a press kit varies. For example, if you go to a top New York agency to design and produce your press kit, you may spend $10,000 or more. However, if you do it yourself, it may cost you around $100 to $250. The cost depends on what you're looking for and where you are in your business. You can spend more, or you can spend less. Keep in mind that if you're spending six figures for your press kit, you should be getting some PR representation as well.

If you don't have a press kit for your business, it limits you. What a press kit does is it gives you accessibility. It's ready. This is critical. Opportunities may come up and you want to be prepared. You don't have time to go home and spend 2-3 days figuring out what you should put in your press kit. You need to be able to say, "Go to my website, click on the media link and download my press kit."

When I had a radio show for a few years, I loved it when people would approach me about my press kit, I would say to them, "Just go to my website, it is right there." Instead of saying, "I'll get my press kit to you next week."

Being prepared is the key to your media success. You'll lose opportunities if you're not ready with your press kit. Also, revisit your press kit every couple of months to make sure it's up-to-date. Get rid of anything that may no longer apply to your press kit.

To make your press kit stand out online, everything is about SEO (search engine optimization). Your keywords should be in the title of your press kit, press release and other documents. Remember, media people search the Internet. If they're looking to interview an expert in your field, you want to make sure your business comes up in the searches.

You'll want to get started with speaking. This way you'll have a few local speaking credits to add to your name. If a journalist, reporter or producer sees that you've spoken to various groups or at events, they'll be more inclined to interview you. Also, take advantage of press release sites such as PR Web. You'll be put into the mix – it will be easier for the media to find and call you.

Another way to stand out is tie-in to some current event. This is known as newsjacking, where you capitalize on the popularity of a news story. Journalists and reporters are always looking for material around a current topic. So... you'd be a fit in the five minute spot. To find out what is current, look at the hashtags on Twitter or trending topics. Watching your daily news will tell you what is "hot" right now. However, you must know how to position yourself and get into that sweet spot to ensure that you're chosen for an interview.

All it takes is a little extra effort to be successful. Everyone else will do something average. If you go a little further than the average, you will be noticed.

You can also send your press kit to targeted "niche" media. For example, if you are a carpenter and you wanted to be known as the next Ty Pennington formerly of *Extreme Makeover Home Edition* and *Trading Spaces*, you would find media places that are speaking about your topic. Search for radio shows, print and online magazines, you name it, and send your press kit out. Get on their radar!

If you send your press kit via email, write an attention grabbing subject line. You want to differentiate yourself from everyone else, so take a moment and think about what makes you different – how do you stand out from the crowd? Keep your email short! Consider taking a clip from an audio or video piece and put it in the email, but include the attachment or link. Wait about 24 hours and then follow up via phone and/or email.

Use a spreadsheet program to keep track of the media you've contacted. If you don't hear anything straightaway or for a few weeks, don't get discouraged. Follow up in six months and keep reaching out. If you knock on enough doors, someone will open one of them.

You may consider going to live events, like trade shows, where media people will be. Shake somebody's hand, look them in the eye and have a conversation. Get to know them on human-to-human level. Find out what they're up to and if you would be a good fit for any segments. Come from a place of wanting to help them fill the spot.

The biggest thing to do is get out of your own way. Some people feel like "I'm nobody. Who am I to have a press kit?" But, really what the mindset you should have is that a press kit is a door opener. If you wait until you're famous to have one, you won't need it! A press kit is a stepping stone to becoming known. Don't take that feeling of "I'm just a nobody; I don't know anyone or anything. I'm not a personality." Well… A press kit is how you get there. Go ahead and position yourself! Here's a story to inspire you:

My brother was a pharmacist and lost his job. He was tired of the corporate game, so I sat down with him and asked, "What do you love to do?" He said, "BBQ!" We talked about it, and he has positioned himself as a BBQ media personality. His website is BBQSuperstars.com. He ordered a couple of shirts with a logo, got a video camera, and reached out to an event and stated that he wanted to cover the BBQ event and put it up on his website on YouTube. Of course, the event people were okay with this.

See what happens when you "claim" something as yours and follow through? Everything unfolds naturally. Today, he has 15,000 hits per month on his blog and growing, in addition to radio shows. Plus, YouTube contacted him and asked to put affiliate ads on his channel, so he's earning income from his videos.

Don't be afraid to create a press kit! Go do those interviews and be the person you know you want to be. Find your passion, what makes you want to get out of bed in the morning, and stick with it.

*****

A SMORGASBORD OF AFFORDABLE PR

Melody L. Friberg owns her own consulting, writing and grant development services business in Northern California.

It's been said that there's no such thing as a free lunch. But there are some free, or fairly nominally priced, sources of publicity for you and your events out there, if you know where to look. This is especially important if you're a sole proprietor, and particularly so, if you're a *new* business owner.

But first things first.

If you've read Christina's book *Media Magnetism* and subscribe to her blog, you already know the basics of successful marketing: developing and practicing a pitch you can deliver on a moment's notice; establishing yourself as an expert in your field; creating a media-ready press kit; and building strong relationships with the media.

But what if you're really new at this entrepreneurial adventure? Short on experience but long on enthusiasm and dreams? If so, consider the joys of volunteering your services or products to gain some valuable "real life" experience. You'll be doing something for the greater good as well as growing your resume and expertise at the same time. Are you new at grant writing? Then volunteer to write grants for nonprofit agencies such as animal rescue groups. Are

161

you a budding music writer? Try donating some of your demonstration CDs to charities holding silent auctions for gift baskets at fundraising events. If you're planning to write the Great American Novel, you could apply your writing skills to non-profit, school, or church newsletters. Do you want to break into public relations? Publicize events for non-profits or for-profit organizations, and gain some experience while learning the PR business at the same time. Experience is experience—its value to you does not depend on whether it's paid or *pro bono*.

Now, on to the free - or almost free - buffet.

I'm using my hometown newspaper and local media to illustrate. Hopefully, you have similar venues where you do business.

Consider the following:

- Contact your newspaper's "small business writer" to interview you.
- Contact your newspaper's journalist who writes about fund-raising events for charities, if your business is a non-profit or your business could co-sponsor a charity event with a non-profit.
- Place announcements of all your events in the "community events section" of your local newspaper.
- Contact your local TV channels' community reporters, morning shows, etc., to discuss how your business serves the community, the value of your products and services, etc.
- Research and contact radio stations (including national public radio) which have talk shows that may find your business a subject of interest to their listeners.
- Contact neighborhood newspapers/magazines (usually given out free at local businesses), and let them know you have an interesting story about your business in the community. Have the article ready to send or email them (you already have several in your media package).

- Contact the local magazine dedicated to your city or region. Oftentimes these magazines take advertising from businesses with photos of the principles.
- Make your business more visible through ads in business-related print media. Offer to write articles on issues affecting the economy or society, and how your business fits in. Place ads in publications your clients might read.
- Advertise in the telephone book and on Craig's List.
- Create YouTubes that showcase your music, your writing, your services, your products, or your expertise. The more exposure you can generate, the better. In the YouTubes, you can provide the message yourself, or have someone else do it for you. Or, perhaps you could develop a slideshow with musical background to illustrate your products or services. You might consider interviews with, or quotes from, satisfied customers; or you could provide testimonials from individuals who have seen and appreciated your talents or products.
- Sponsor seminars on specific themes. For example, if you provide services for the homeless, offer a seminar with advocates, non-profits that are well-known in the community for serving that population, government agencies that can discuss legal/regulatory issues, and city/county requirements to provide services.
- Provide a survey to your established or *potential* client base to identify their needs, obstacles to using your services, etc. As a thank-you for participation, enter them in a drawing for a free consultation or product samples.
- Pursue new collaboration opportunities with organizations that complement the services you provide; i.e., government agencies, schools, job training programs.

- Seek out large corporations or businesses that might consider paying you for your services to help their own philanthropic interests, target populations and employees. Religious groups may also have charitable interests, and your business might provide them with what they need to pursue those interests.

This smorgasbord is open to everyone. Be creative, and stay hungry!

*****

BE YOUR OWN PRODUCER!

Shari Stauch, creator of Where Writers Win, has been involved in publishing and marketing for 30 years, first for individual athletes, and now for authorpreneurs.

There are so many fantastic and free promotional tools available for sole proprietors these days, especially when it comes to pushing out content. Chances are you're already your own in-house PR firm, advertising agency, publisher, and more. You should be using every resource at your disposal to its best advantage to establish yourself as an expert in whatever service or product you have to offer to the masses.

Sharing content begins with your website and blog. If you don't have a blog integrated with your website, get one. It's the area that keeps your site "in motion" and that will change regularly enough to keep your website fresh and continually searched and indexed by search engines. It's the place you can share insights, promotions, tips or whatever else may be of interest to your customers. And they can subscribe to get the latest updates, giving you an easy place to build an email list and distribute to it.

From there you may want to explore other written content pieces you can produce, e.g. white papers (PDFs of collected info, such as a "best of" selection of your articles or blog posts) or e-books. E-books tend to be larger collections of information (say 32 pages or more). You can give away your white papers or e-books as an incentive for signing up for your email list. You can also put them up for sale at popular sites such as Amazon's Kindle, Barnes & Noble, etc., to gain even more attention.

Once you have the written communication strategy down, you'll want to consider audio or video content to really soup up your marketing. Technology today allows practically anyone to launch an audio or video podcast, build a commercial or even do a regular video series on YouTube. For sole proprietors, this is an incredible opportunity for tooting your own horn and being a media star!

Establishing yourself as the credible authority to potential clients requires deciding how –and where – you'll share your knowledge. Happily for the "how," producing podcasts and videos is easier than ever thanks to computers with built-in programs and a variety of online resources to get you started. To begin, Google "How to make a podcast" or "How to make an audio podcast" and you'll find dozens of answers and free resources.

Hint: Even if you've had experience with audio or video podcasts, you'll want to do this online search. Resources and methods change as technology improves, and it will be to your ultimate benefit to have the latest information to save you time, money and probably a lot of aggravation.

Once you've decided on "the method," you'll want to get the most mileage out of it, or to be blunt, "the madness." That means finding new and creative ways to get your podcasts or videos heard and seen by potential customers. Here are seven ideas to get you started once you've shared on your own website:

1. ITunes is a great place to upload your podcast, as is Podomatic.com, where you can create and broadcast your podcast. ITunes offers plenty of free podcasts, as well as subscription models, should you decide to monetize your productions. BlogTalkRadio.com lets you create your own radio show, a more regularly scheduled sort of podcast that you can use to develop a following. Other popular online radio show sites include TalktainmentRadio.com and TalkZone.com. Hint: Search for podcasts and radio shows in your industry to learn what channels others are using. You might even find outlets where you can be a guest or guest host!

2. YouTube.com - The most obvious outlet for video is YouTube. Once you've uploaded your video there, it's also easy to share it to a number of places, embed it on your website, etc. Google and YouTube will help you through every step of the way with plenty of FAQs and tutorials.

3. DailyMotion.com - Another of the biggest video platforms in the world with 120 million monthly unique visitors (Comscore, 2013) generating over 2.5 billion video views every month. Dailymotion is the most popular European site, too. It's quick, easy and free to create an account (you can log in with Facebook) and upload a video.

4. Don't forget to share links to your audio/video on social media sites. Give yourself a reminder - perhaps one week on Facebook, another on Twitter, Google Plus, Linked In, Pinterest, etc. By scattering the posts, you'll cast a wide net of potential views. And, while we don't advocate spamming your customers, it doesn't hurt to re-post once in a while. Existing readers will ignore it (like we do all those Coca Cola

commercials) but new readers will have a chance to view and may share with others.

5. Friends and colleagues with websites are an overlooked option. Get together with other business owners in your community or within your area of expertise and share each other's videos on your websites and social media outlets.

6. PhotoBucket.com - Not just for photos, this highly social and mobile-friendly site allows for uploads of both photos and videos, so you can show off your store, products or even your latest headshot.

7. Does your video fit the theme of a movie playing at your local theater? Many local movie theaters also run local ad content; offer them your video for a fun alternative. Local interest pricing is often more reasonable than you think, and a great way to create buzz and "test the waters" of a paid promotion without breaking the bank.

Finally, keep in mind that a good producer always keeps his/her audience in mind. Produce content that is interesting and engaging and you'll find it easy to create a following of eager readers, listeners and viewers!

BE OUR GUEST

In the academic world, college professors are encouraged to publish scholarly titles as a way to perpetuate their status as experts. In the business world, blogs fulfill a less formal but just as important game-plan to put an author's name in front of an audience and keep it in circulation. What began as a form of online journaling in the 1990's has grown to over 30 million bloggers in the United States. According to Blogging.org, 60 percent of businesses have now made routine blogging part of their marketing platform. Is it part of yours? If not, what are you waiting for?

For starters, you don't have to be a savvy wordsmith or a techno geek to hop on this free marketing platform. If you know how to spot trends, upload pictures, and keep your content short, engaging and meaningful on a regular basis, in no time at all you can build a following, a following that could transition to buyers of whatever your business is selling. Surveys have shown that people are more likely to purchase goods and services from companies and individuals that they feel they already "know" and feel comfortable with. When your name and your blogs repeatedly pop up in search engines for topics that people want to know more about, you're not only building credibility as an expert in your field but also growing your company brand without a hard-sell approach.

No one likes to feel as if they're being hit up for a sale and yet that's often what happens when beginning bloggers treat the experience as if it's an aggressive commercial. To me, this is little different from when I ask someone a question for a feature interview and they say, "Oh, it's all on my website" (which seems to have become the electronic equivalent of, "Oh, it's all in my book"). In other words, "I don't actually have time to answer what you just asked me but I think you should make the time to go troll for it yourself. And, by the way, buy something from me while you're there."

A guest blog is an enticement, a tease, a snappy sound-bite that encourages readers to want to know what *else* you know that could be helpful to them. While it can contain a brief bio and website link at the end – and many blog hosts allow this – the blog itself should never come across as brazenly self-promotional. It is, instead, an earned media opportunity to express what you think, to invite conversation through comments, and to share resources and recommendations with kindred spirits. If, for instance, someone says, "I really like all these restaurant reviews and recipes that Tony writes about. This guy really knows food!"…and then notices in the bio that Tony is the author of a cookbook and the publisher of a foodie magazine, they'll feel as if they have just made a remarkable discovery on their own without Tony ever hawking either one.

Did you know that penning guest blogs for others as well as inviting them to reciprocate is a way to turn your competitors into your collaborators? If you embrace an isolationist mindset that you don't want to spotlight the accomplishments of a fellow life coach because it might take potential customers away from your own life coach business, you're ignoring the basic principle that "we're all in this together." You're also ignoring a valuable opportunity to increase your Internet footprint. Cooperative blogosity built on mutual respect can subsequently lead to customer referrals, co-authoring books together, trading invitations to speaking engagements and yes, long-term friendships, too.

And who knows? The discipline of committing to a new blog (whether it's twice a week or once a month) can lead you to become a more introspective thinker, a more attentive listener, a more-rounded observer of the world around you, and even a more focused and better writer – any one of which will be a bonus to your business and your life.

*****

REACH YOUR AUDIENCE WITH GUEST
BLOGGING

Danny Iny, a.k.a. the "Freddy Krueger of Blogging", is the proud founder of Firepole Marketing.

After recovering from the fact that a previous startup had disintegrated all around me and imploded as a result of the markets crashing, I was rebuilding a consulting practice and was doing okay. But I was trading time for money in a very direct way. There's nothing inherently wrong with this, I found out that I was bumping up against a very low ceiling about how far I could go or grow. The better I did, the less time, energy and resources I had left over to grow any further. I was hitting the limits on the model I was in, at least the way I was doing it.

I started looking to the online world as a way of being a little more leveraged, a little more diversified, finding something that will support other people. In doing that and casting around, I looked at the experience of having working with people in my local area; the consulting that I've been doing was kind of marketing and strategy consulting serving small business owners and entrepreneurs with 0-10 employee range. I found that there were plenty of people who were in that bracket and needed my services. But there were a lot of people in that segment that were kind of just getting started that were struggling and needed a lot of help, but couldn't afford to pay for it.

I gave a lot of my time away for free, which was fine, because when I was getting started a lot of people helped me out. You want to pay it forward. However, my time didn't scale and there were more people to help then I really had the time to help. So I thought to myself, *Hey! Isn't there an opportunity here to create some kind of an online program for them and reach the millions of millions of people on the internet?* I did what I now teach online students not to do, which is spend a ton of time, like over 2,000 hours, building this enormous training program and it was all stuff that I thought they needed to know. It's a great program for what it is: an introductory to marketing, everything you need to know about marketing to be a competent marketer. The trouble is it's what I thought they needed. But it's not what they were looking for or wanted. Hardly anyone bought the program, and I ended up retiring the product and moved on to more successful products.

Having built my marketing program, I wondered how I would get the word out about it. How would I get people aware of this? I set up a blog, and I experimented with a few different strategies online and came to guest posting. That's where we initially experienced a lot of explosive growth. People suddenly started to know me over the internet. I kind of became, over the course of maybe a year, this low-level D-List, or maybe even C-Plus List celebrity within the online world.

What is Guest Blogging?

There are many blogs on the internet, and blogs are basically like online magazines. They publish new articles, whatever frequency they publish, whether it's daily, weekly, a few times a week. Blog owners publish new content and people come and read it. People subscribe to it much as they subscribe to a magazine.

Guest blogging is just like writing an article for a magazine. Pitching an article to a blog owner, and if they like it, they will publish it for you. What this allows you to do is reach a whole bunch of people who are reading that magazine, that blog. It's weirdly counterintuitive for people to understand. They feel that since they're creating content they should put it on their blog. It never occurs to them why write all this content for your blog if you don't have any readers. It's like creating newsletter every month but you're not sending it to anyone. Instead of that, create content and reach out to blog owners who have a significant readership and get it published there.

Even though you may not get paid to write a guest post (some blog owners may pay you a fee), it's marketing. Think about this. No one will pay you to put together your brochure or website, it's the same thing. The only difference is that people will see your posts. This has impact and is valuable. It's no different than being published in a magazine or newspaper.

Obviously you don't want to give *everything* away for free. The idea is to connect with strangers who don't know you. The first impression they get is that they get to learn something and from there they can move on to a more engaged relationship.

Benefits and Drawbacks of Guest Blogging

There are three categories of benefits of guest blogging:

- **Traffic** – In other words, many people read major blogs. They will read the content and click through the links back to your website and discover you. People find you for the first time.

- **Credibility** – There's implied credibility by being featured on major blogs. It says implicitly that these blogs trust you. For example, if someone reads your post on Forbes.com that tells the reader that you're someone they should listen to. You can also take the logos of these websites and put them on your website in an "As Featured On" section because you've legitimately have been.
- **Relationship** – The most valuable benefit of all! This is a good way to get your foot in the door and starting to build relationships with the owners of these blogs and that's huge.

There are also three categories of drawbacks to guest blogging.

- **Time and Work** – It takes time to be a guest blogger. You have to put in the time to create good content and do the outreach to blog owners. It takes work to be a guest blogger. Not only do you have to put in the time to write guest blog posts, you have to think of unique angles to topics that have already be written by other bloggers.
- **Rejection** – Your guest blog pitches may be rejected by blog owners. But don't let this discourage you from pitching your content ideas. While blog owners may reject your posts, for whatever reason, others will accept them.
- **Return is Linear** – You're putting in a big chunk of your time, and the returns may not be huge at first, but you're building a foundation of reputation. That has aggregate value over time. Once you guest post for a certain amount of time, you'll build your audience and become a recognized authority in your field.

Guest blogging is a powerful stepping tool to get to somewhere. It can also be a useful tool to continue to move places, if that's your strategy. But it doesn't necessarily have to be. Doing guest blogging well doesn't mean you have to keep doing it forever.

Steps to Becoming a Guest Blogger

It's very easy to become a guest blogger. You find the blogs within your industry that you read. Extensively, you're serving people like you to a certain degree. However, you can go to the blogs that your customers read. If you don't know the blogs that your customers read, you may want to consider that you may be out-of-touch with your customers. You'll need to know your customers better. There's a certain amount of know your own industry.

You can look at blog directories, for example, Technorati. You can also search top blogs (fill in the blank industry). You can get in touch with authorities within your industry and interview them for your blog, which is a good way to get your foot in the door for a conversation with them. You can then ask them, "Who are the authorities you look at? What blogs do you read?" You must understand your market.

When you find blogs within your industry, spend time reading and studying them. Look at the content that gets published. What is the tone? What is the style? What types of content does well on the blogs? What posts are shared the most often? What generates the most conversation? What is the most popular content? Ultimately, blogs are in the business of publishing content that people are going to enjoy. You want to know what that is.

Approaching Blog Owners

Do not reach out cold. You don't want to send an email where you write, "Hey! You never heard of me, but..." This is not a good way of starting a conversation with anyone. After you've taken the time to read the content on the blog and got to know the community, start commenting. Most blogs have a feature that allows you to leave a comment on what you've read. You want to leave engaging substantive comments – that you have something worthwhile to say. If you do that for a while, people will start to notice.

Note: If blog owners have guest blog guidelines published, you may cold email. However, as a rule, it's always better not to cold email.

Keep in mind that blog owners of large blogs get

approached numerous times throughout the year. You want to build a relationship first before you start reaching out to them.

Virality of a Guest Blog Post

The hope that a guest blog post will go viral is a pipe dream. For example, your idea that once you publish a post it will be shared 4,000 times and 200,000 people will see it probably will not happen. You may have some relative hits. But remember that virality exists on a spectrum. It's not either viral or not, it's more or less viral. Guest blogging is not about getting one *magic* homerun. It's about consistent effort.

Structure of Guest Blog Post

You want to open a blog post with a hook, which is a short description of either the pain that the reader is currently experiencing or the pleasure they want but don't have. You're talking about how to choose an outcome because you're teaching them something. What are the symptoms of their current reality? From there, you'll explain the problems they see. In other words, what do they see as the cause of these symptoms? This is important because, if they were right, they would have solved the problem. However, you know something they don't. After you acknowledge their perspective on what might be causing their problem, there's a deeper layer. What's the root of the problem? You explain that, and then you can move to talk about a solution and call-to-action (CTA). You show/tell readers what they can do next, which may involve implementing something you talk about. Or you may direct them to your website to check out (fill in the blank), so that you may help them.

You may or may not include media in your guest blog post. For example, some guest bloggers incorporate images from beginning to end, while others embed audio or video. Media isn't necessary, but is worthwhile if you have good and appropriate media. Make sure you have the copyright to use media.

While the above structure is meant to be a guideline, it's important to know and follow the structure of the blogs you want to guest post for. This is why it's important to spend time on blogs to see which posts have done well. You want to learn from and emulate the content that has been the most successful on blogs because that's what readers respond to.

Headlines Matter

You want to spend enough time on headlines so that you don't trivialize them. Headlines determine whether people are going to click and actually read blog posts. You want to put effort into your headlines. A good way to come up with headlines is to look at the most successful blog posts on blogs. Pay attention to the structure of the headlines. Often, they follow the same basic structure. For example, a list post may be "A Number (choose a number) of Ways to (Fill in the Blank) By Doing Something Else." A metaphor based headline, for example, "What's (Fill in the Blank) One Thing Can Teach You about (Fill in the Blank)." There are a lot of permutations on these formulas. You can look at these formulas. However, there are three guidelines in writing good headlines, which come from Sean D'Souza at Psycho Tactics. They are:

- A good headline is going to be questioned based, not answered based.
- A good headline is going to be problem based, not solution based.
- A good headline will arouse curiosity.

You can't always hit all three of these in headlines. But aim for at least one or two.

How Many Guest Posts Could You Write?

You want to write as many guest posts as you can! There isn't a right or wrong answer. Write as many guest posts as you have time to create. Some people think that it may be easy, that you can write a couple of guest posts a month and you're done. However, if this is a significant marketing strategy you're employing, you'll want to write many guest posts, maybe 80 or more or whatever that number is for you. Also, you may write for your blog too.

176

But remember that if your blog is not attracting your audience, yet, it's better to guest blog on large blogs that have a built-in audience.

Yes, guest posting is a lot of time and work, but it's not about that. It's about getting the results that you want, whatever those are.

It's critical to be consistent with guest posting. Shoot for one blog post a week. Otherwise, your progress is going to be very slow. Two a month is very little and it's a lot better than nothing. But it's very little. Ideally, one or two a week is the frequency in which you should be writing. At first, this will take a lot of time. As you get better, it will speed up.

The key in terms of the division of where you're posting is to aim for 50-70% of your blog posts to be targeted at the blogs where you got the best results in the past, and 30-50% are on new blogs that you're adding to the mix to see how they perform.

A blog that has a good readership and where you do a good job with your blog posts, with the call-to-action at the bottom that takes people to your website where they can learn more about you, you may get between 50-150 new email list subscribers. In other words, let's say 200, 300, maybe even 400 people go back to your website and check out what you're doing. This is if you're doing a good job and on the right blogs. It may take you time to find what those places and locations are.

Bear in mind that you do not want to repurpose guest blog posts, even though they may have done well on blogs. The general expectation that people have is you own the intellectual property, it's your article. But, you're granting blog owners exclusive licenses to publish your posts. However, you may take your posts and publish them in a book where people can't find it on blogs. You should be okay. But remember that this is not legal advice, and you may consider consulting with an attorney for further clarification on licensing.

Blogging with Gusto

To learn more about guest blogging, you may consider taking an online class. At the end of the day there is an opportunity cost to doing this and not doing it properly.

If you go after the wrong blogs, you won't get good results. The relatively trivial amount of money that it costs to do it right would be money well spent.

When you first start guest blogging, you may face obstacles, the biggest being one of confidence. You may think guest blogging is harder than it really is which may lead you to resist reaching out to blog owners. Don't let this hold you back. Find blogs within your industry, read and comment on them, and then pitch blog owners.

Guest blogging is an interesting venue to explore ideas, to flush out what you know and share it with others. It's rewarding to put that information, those ideas, in places where there are going to be a lot of people reading, seeing, interacting and appreciating it. It's a nice change of pace from writing and saving it on your hard drive and hoping you have an opportunity to show it to someone. And remember the old expression... If you don't make time for marketing, pretty soon you'll have lots of time for marketing!

RUBICONS AND BURNOUTS

When you're on the cusp of an exciting new venture – a marriage, a dream job, a perfect house – "How am I going to get out of this?" is probably the farthest question from your mind. With the exception of certain politicians who spend their entire term campaigning for re-election (or the next higher office), most people approach each of these unfolding chapters with the expectation of settling in for the long-term and being happy as a clam. When you're bright-eyed and effusive with optimism – and especially when you're a solo business owner – it's rarely in your wheelhouse to consider things like exit strategies on the very first day you hang out a shingle. Yet given the number of elements that can impact both your professional sustainability and your personal growth, it's never too early to take a long view of where that path could eventually lead you…and whether you'll want to stay on it.

In the summer of 1978, I started a touring theater company. The common assumption was that it represented a transition from acting to directing/producing. The true agenda, however, was to address a longstanding problem I had observed from years of treading the boards in community and college productions; specifically, the practice of directors always casting the same actors in every show. As I often told people, landing your first role in a play is not unlike getting your first credit card. Everyone would love to give you one as long as someone else has already proven you're a good risk. Despite all the training I was providing aspiring thespians on how to ace an audition, directors tended to look with disdain on anyone who showed up at try-outs with an empty resume. One such person I had formerly worked with even went so far as to say, "My shows are much too important to risk on unknowns." Since I saw the creative potential of the enthusiastic newbies in my workshops, the obvious test of what I was teaching them about the craft of acting was to start my own troupe and cast them myself in a diverse range of roles to hone their skills on stage.

Was it challenging? Yes. Was it sometimes vexatiously crazy? Yes. Was it gloriously fun? Yes, yes, a thousand times yes. Not only was I accomplishing what I'd set out to do by opening doors that had previously been closed to fledgling actors but the company was also providing a platform to develop my playwriting expertise. "I could do this forever," I remember thinking.

Until I hit the 8-year mark.

The inciting incident was catching the worst cold and sore throat of my life. Although I wasn't contagious, I felt wretched. Further, I was acting in one of the productions and my voice was about to go out at any moment. I turned to my assistant director and told her that she might have to go on in my place. Instead of sympathy, I got indignation. "You're not supposed to get sick!" she shot back.

Apparently I must have missed that memo.

Perhaps it's because I always made everything look effortless (which it truly wasn't), I was never supposed to get sick, be tired, need a break or take a vacation. As is often the case when you're the boss of your own business, the line between a work life and a home life gets so fuzzily blurred that you wake up one day and realize it's not a healthy pattern to continue indefinitely (no matter how much you loved it at the beginning). I had also reached a point of starting to assess which one of the three things I did best – acting, directing and writing – would have the longest (and most portable) shelf life.

The subsequent decision to focus 100 percent on my writing meant that the show, sadly, would have to go on without me. Having already trained a handful of assistant directors to lighten the rehearsal load, I approached them with the idea of their collectively continuing the company after my departure. The reaction was unanimous: "It's too much work." While many of my actors were happily treading the boards in productions all across town, there were just as many still with me who felt my decision was selfish. "How can you end something you yourself started?" they asked. There were even those who equated "quitting" with "failure," despite eight years of success. The latter, I think, especially applies to the mindset of any sole proprietor who – following the hoopla of a grand opening – realizes one day that they're just no longer passionate about baking designer cupcakes, doing consulting, or publishing other authors' ebooks.

The answer is that everything which ends means the start of something new. And in the end, taking a step out of your comfort zone and off a familiar path can lead to destinations you never imagined possible.

*****

HOW PERSISTENCE IN YOUR LIFE AND BUSINESS GETS YOU WHAT YOU WANT EVERY TIME

Diane Conklin, President and Founder of Complete Marketing Systems, is an internationally known author, entrepreneur, coach, consultant and speaker.

Ever notice how life seems to get in the way?

Really…

How many times have you set a goal, or started the day with the best intentions and then everything seemed to fall apart? From the very beginning of the day your plan got off track…and it stayed that way all day. We've all had those days, and sometimes, it feels like we have those weeks…or months. It happens in business and in your aspects of your life.

So, the question becomes how do you get it all done? How do you start or run a successful business, have a relationship with all the significant people in your life, throw in a little fun once in a while, and have a life?

There is no one single answer to this age old question that seems to grow even more pressing and urgent every single day…even with all the technology that's supposed to help us leverage our time.

Have you ever noticed how so many things that are supposed to make our lives better just make them more complicated? For example, when tablets came out, they were supposed to allow us to travel without our laptops. Instead, what happened was that now we have more gadgets. Observe the next time you go on a trip and see what people travel with. It will look something like this: a laptop, a tablet, a book reader of some kind, a real book or books, a smart phone, an iPod, all the chargers and plugs and cords to go with all this, and it ends up being more, not less.

It's like that in business sometimes too. While you have to stay on top of technology and trends, sometimes, reverting back to the basics of what works and what has always worked just makes things simpler and keeps the fun alive.

More important than almost anything else is that you measure what you're doing in your business so you know what's working and what isn't, so you can do what works and stop doing what doesn't.

While that sounds logical and makes perfect sense, so many business owners don't measure anything in their business – and if they do know any of their numbers it's not the ones that matter the most.

Do you know what it costs you to get a new client? Or, what the ROI (Return On Investment) of your last campaign was?

How do you learn all the things you need to know to run a successful business anyway? What should you be measuring? How do you do all the things that need to be done, and most importantly, how to make money in the ever changing world we live and work in?

This is where persistence comes into play.

Running a successful business isn't a one-time event. The only "overnight success" is in other people's minds. There are always a lot of behind the scenes things going on that only the business owner sees. All the outside world sees is the glamour and the success. The hard work, long hours, tough decisions, failures, challenges, heart-ache and struggles happen in the back room where nobody sees them...but they happen all the same. They always do.

One of the biggest mistakes business owners make – ones just starting out as well as those who have been in business for a long time – is drawing a line in the sand and saying something like "If this (fill in the blank) doesn't happen by this date" or "If I don't make this much money by this time" and then you end the statement with something like "I'm going to quit" or "I'm going to get a job."

It's during the times when you feel this way that you have to turn to the reason you do what you do and the reason you started your business in the first place.

The problem with drawing the proverbial line in the sand is that you don't know when success (however you define it) will come, or what it will look like exactly.

How do you know if the next thing you do is the thing

that will catapult you over the edge to the success you've always dreamed of?

What if your big break is the phone call that's coming your way?

What if tomorrow is your day, or next week?

You just have to persist through whatever challenge is in your way. Challenges are just put there to see how tough you are, to see if you'll find a way through, over, under or around it...or if you'll quit. Persistence doesn't mean you keep doing the same things over and over again if they aren't working – that's the definition of insanity! Persistence means if one door doesn't open, you try the next one, and the next one, and the one after that...until you find an open door – or the key to unlock one, or somebody walks out of that locked door and you can slip in.

It just means you don't quit.

Persistence also doesn't mean you have to barrel your way through things. Try just leaning into them instead. One step at a time is how things get done. It's also how you conquer your fears. Sometimes, you have to take baby steps. And, you almost always have to take baby steps before you can walk and you have to walk before you can run!

Finally, remember to be flexible. Almost nothing turns out the way it looks in our heads.

Make a plan, but be flexible to changing, taking a different path, or starting over even, if that's what it takes.

No matter where you are in your process, your race, or your part of the game of life and business, remember to keep going. It's worth it!

*****

LOST THAT LOVING FEELING? – 10 TIPS TO HELP YOU REIGNITE YOUR PASSION FOR YOUR BUSINESS

Jennifer Martin is a published author, business coach, and the founder of Zest Business Consulting.

So you're burnt out, you feel like you don't have a life, and something inside of you feels missing or broken. You spend all this time finally making your business dream come true and as much as you hate to face the facts, you've lost that loving feeling. Is it time to throw in the towel? Or, is there another way you can get back on track?

No one ever said that being a sole proprietor was going to be easy, but it can be tremendously rewarding. As an entrepreneur you get to make choices every day, from where you work to what hours you are available and who your clients are. You have the freedom to be who you are and follow your heart. But the problem is that most of us never learned how to do business this way.

It's never too late to rekindle your passion. Here are some tips to help you get your mojo back.

1. Fire your old boss (the part of you that forgot how to have fun) and hire yourself a new supervisor (again this would be you) who treats you like they really care. What can you today do to start treating yourself with the patience, kindness, consideration, and support you would give to someone on your team?

2. Take control of your relationship with your business. If in the past your business was like an "unhealthy" or toxic partner, then it's time you traded up. Reestablish the role you play at work and determine what you need to do keep things healthy and interesting. If you decide to show up differently, your business won't hold you to being the person you were in the past. From this point forward, think meaningful, fun, and soul-satisfying.

3. Rediscover your "why." Chances are you aren't exactly the same person now as you were when you first started your business. So, it's important to check in every so often to reconnect with why you're doing what you do, beyond the money. Start by giving serious thought to (WIIFM) What's In It For Me? Do you enjoy working from home in your bathrobe? Are you helping make people's lives more enjoyable? Are you following your heart doing something that you love? Let the positive "whys" reignite your passion for your business.

4. Practice saying "No" and set boundaries with your time. Remember, just because you can "do it," doesn't mean you have. Reach out for support when you can, and be willing to say no to anything that isn't essential. You don't get extra points for trying to be a superhero and doing it all. Reinvent your life so that you can be at your best.

5. Commit yourself to fun. Reinvent your job around what you think is fun and delegate the rest. Schedule more fun in your life and don't forget to take a vacation! Of course there are 101 things on your "to do" list, but that doesn't mean that doing them will actually make a difference on your bottom line. Stay focused on what you love about doing what you do and keep it interesting every day.

6. Celebrate your successes and reward yourself for what you've accomplished. When good things happen for you and your business, it's essential you CELEBRATE! So that you won't forget how amazing you are, keep a Small Success Journal and track the good things that are happening (when you get positive feedback from a customer, you close a new deal, you make progress on a project that at one point felt insurmountable, etc.). Read your journal daily and add to it as you notice new accomplishments and successes worth remembering. This can be a great way to stay upbeat and notice that you are moving, step by step closer to your goal.

7. Declutter and get rid of everything that isn't a good fit. You'll be surprised by how much energy a whiny client sucks out of you. Why get stuck in the same old habit or patterns? Clean your desk top, your file cabinet, and your e-mail inbox and then move on to letting go of stuff you no longer need. Don't be afraid to let go of clients you don't love and anyone that isn't living up to your expectations. Clear out the junk that doesn't serve you and make room for more of what you want.

8. Make balance your middle name. If you want to show up with the best you have to offer, you have to take care of yourself on a regular basis. Schedule at least 30 minutes of personal time for yourself every day and discover what would bring more balance to your life.

9. Spice it up! Don't get stuck in the same old routines. Consider setting your schedule so it mirrors your internal body clock. If you can't seem to get anything done from your office then try working somewhere else. Try moving your desk to the other side of the office. Keep your work-life vibrant and interesting.

10. If you need help staying on track you don't have to go it alone. Find a peer group, a mentor, or a coach to help

you feel like you have a community of support moving forward.

It is entirely possible to have a successful business and a vibrant meaningful life. Many of the keys to success are right here waiting for you to dig on in. The real question is: What are you going to do now? For today, imagine that you've got what it takes to achieve your dreams and goals. It's time you gave yourself permission to THRIVE!

*****

EXPECT THE UNEXPECTED

Australian and French Quarterite style-setter, artist, and community activist Dianne Harris is CEO of tour de force eclectic boutique Oonkas Boonkas.

When you're a sole proprietor, you not only have to be ready to put yourself out there, do things you've never done, and overcome obstacles no one ever warned you about but you also have to try something new *every single day*. With an ailing economy and consumer confidence at an all-time low, you have to be more strategic than ever by locking in a solid business plan, becoming a tenacious catalyst for change, and recognizing you should only consider it time to pull the pin if confronted with forces far greater than you are.

It's often said you get just one big chance to get it right. Mine came from running away with the circus. A chance meeting at Cirque Du Soleil led to a love affair that spanned the globe and - two days after eloping in Las Vegas - a business was born. Neither of us was employed and with a new apartment to pay the note on, we braved rain, hail and shine pushing a makeshift rack down the middle of the road to The French Market in New Orleans where we began selling vintage decorated cowboy hats. It was a vibrant, multi-layered culture like no other, and after 15 months of trading outside, setting up each day in the elements, and expanding our inventory, our first boutique's doors opened on Rue St Philip. Oonkas Boonkas continued to go from strength to strength, only to suffer a huge set-back three years later in the summer of 2005.

186

In a heartbeat, our lives changed forever. When Hurricane Katrina rolled into town and the city filled like a fish bowl, life as we knew it would never be the same again. Our business and community were wiped out. There's quite the story in having fled three hurricanes in a row and ending up in New York in the middle of winter with just the summer clothes and flip-flops we had evacuated New Orleans with three months before.

Eventually when we returned to New Orleans in November the city was still like a war zone and a grey silty mess. Time stood still. Rotting refrigerators in the street. A mountain of rubbish pulled out of the flooded lakefront houses was 10 stories high. It would be another five months before we could think about reopening the shop which had been so damaged by a collapsed ceiling and black mold spreading throughout. I remember vividly the day we secured a new location for our boutique and left a deposit cheque with our new landlord, only to discover that the money - which came from the first payment of our disaster unemployment assistance - had been removed from our account as a $550 fine from Merchant Services for not trading since Katrina. We didn't have money for food and here they were making our landlord's cheque bounce!

I learned a lot about people. Some would take advantage of survivors; others would give you the shirt off their backs. Artists jump-started our city back on its feet by igniting social commentary, marching against escalating crime and generally leading the way to recovery. When I see the vision of New Orleans underwater to this day, it's hard to fathom how we came back from that. We shared experiences both on highs and lows that will bond us together forever. The soul and spirit of New Orleans is in the people that live there. Until you go through a natural disaster of such high proportions, you couldn't possibly understand. It left us with a precious gift to make the most of life and to "live in the moment."

What's the worst that can happen? You lose everything! Then pick yourself up by your bootstraps and rebuild. When you help yourself, others step forward to lend you a hand.

Having seen New Orleans through six years of rebuilding/recovery and weathering the subsequent economic challenges of the BP oil spill and the U.S. economy crash, we felt it was time for a new beginning.

(The safety of home and returning to family and friends in Australia after 10 years of living overseas seemed appealing. Had we stayed in New Orleans, we'd always live with the stress that another Level 5 hurricane could hit us front-on again.)

Little did we know our biggest challenge lay ahead. Luckily our experience through hurricanes had prepared us to have resilient strength to navigate obstacles and bring a once- fractured community together in harmony. Moving from the well-oiled tourism machine that's New Orleans to a local shopping precinct in Melbourne during the recent dramatic changes in retail, we realised we were suddenly dealing with a completely different beast. For the first eight months of our lease we couldn't trade because of entrenched drug and alcohol street-related behaviour which kept shutting us down. Couple this with a high cost of living, sluggish Australia tourism, mass production from China, and commercial shop-front overheads so high you're compelled to work 6-7 days a week. That can be a burden when you want to be creative away from the shop floor! Tying down your talent and leaving you time-poor makes you a slave to the cause.

On the plus side, we discovered our progressive, eclectic brand and retail storytelling style were not only ahead of their trend in Australia but that our focus could be more global than local. I also found that community activism can propel you into enormous personal empowerment and professional growth. When you invest in your community, profound shifts in personal and business potential can happen. At the end of the day, the simplicity of showing care and kindness to your community will rub off and come back to you tenfold in your everyday life. Genuine good Samaritans draw like-minded, positive people. There are networks of community partners willing to engage and work with you to solve issues, create events and bring awareness to your area.

Such was the community advocacy approach we took to collaborate and join together key relationship stakeholders, local traders, law enforcement and city organizations to address the crime issues affecting all of us. Instead of a fractured community, it became a fluid wide network of opportunities. Revitalisation commenced as new businesses moved in and people came from far and wide to

188

experience the hype and media buzz showcasing the new emerging eclectic vibe.

Sometimes events beyond your control can take you on an irreversible journey that wasn't mapped-out in your business plan. The dream you're pursuing can be waylaid by the most unexpected twists and turns. This is when you truly find out what you're made of.

Have I ever been at the point of no return? Yes, countless times. Am I there right now? Absolutely! That's what entrepreneurs do. We wear many hats and try many different approaches when living on the business edge. All you can do is try everything you possibly can to reinvent your situation and - when you manage to get to the other side - you might just surprise yourself. The life and business challenges you encounter along the way will add many more skills to your repertoire.

If you fail your original goal, you might just find you have unearthed an even greater life's purpose.

RESOURCES

BOOKS

Become Your Own Boss in 12 Months: A Month-by-Month Guide to a Business that Works
Author: Melinda F. Emerson
Adams Media (2010)

Be the Red Jacket in a Sea of Gray Suits: The Keys to Unlocking Sales Success
Author: Leanne Hoagland-Smith
Sales Gravy Press (2009)

Business and Baby at Home: A Set-Up and Survival Guide for Mums
Author: Sarah O'Bryan
Finch Publishing (2013)

Connected to Goodness: Manifest Everything You Desire in Business and Life
Authors: David Meltzer and Harrison Lebowitz
Balboa Press (2014)

E-commerce Get It Right! Essential Step-by-Step Guide for Selling & Marketing Products Online
Author: Ian Daniel
NeuroDigital (2011)

Engagement from Scratch
Author: Danny Iny
CreateSpace (2011)

Fired at Fifty: Stop Looking For Work & Discover What You Were Meant To Do
Author: Christine E. Till
Influence Publishing, Inc. (2013)

Great Performances: The Small Business Script for the 21ˢᵗ Century
Author: Clemens Rettich
Influence Publishing Inc. (2012)

Innovation and Entrepreneurship
Author: Peter F. Drucker
Harper Business (2006)

Interactive Ethics: How Ethical and Unethical Decisions Are Really Made in Organizations
Author: Thomas H. Schear
CCMS, Inc. (2014)

Media Magnetism: How to Attract the Favorable Publicity You Want and Deserve
Editor: Christina Hamlett
Outskirts Press (2012)

Small Time Operator: How to Start Your Own Business, Keep Your Books, Pay Your Taxes, and Stay Out of Trouble
Author: Bernard B. Kamoroff
Taylor Trade Publishing (2013)

Surviving the Economy: Practical Tips From Small Business Owners From Around the Globe
Author: Tony Wilkins
CreateSpace/Amazon Independent Publishing Platform (2012)

Telemarketing Success For Small and Mid-Sized Firms
Author: Tony Wilkins
Xlibris, Corp. (2004)

The Entrepreneur Mind: 100 Essential Beliefs, Characteristics, and Habits of Elite Entrepreneurs
Author: Kevin D. Johnson
Johnson Media, Inc. (2013)

The Village Effect: How Face-to-Face Contact Can Make Us Healthier, Happier and Smarter
Author: Susan Pinker
Spiegel and Grau (2014)

12 Tips and Secrets for Authors
Author: Corine La Font
HelpDesk JA (2013)

22 Legal Mistakes You Don't Have to Make: A Guide for Start-ups, Small Businesses, & Tech Entrepreneurs
Author: Sue Wang
Papervine Press (2012)

CONSULTANTS/BUSINESSES/SUPPORT SERVICES

AWeber
http://www.aweber.com

Wendy Anderson
WOW! Event Productions
http://www.woweventproductions.com

Blogger
https://www.blogger.com

Blog Talk Radio
http://www.blogtalkradio.com

Brown Paper Tickets
http://www.brownpapertickets.com

Jeanette Chasworth
The Color Whisperer
http://www.thecolorwhisperer.com

John Churchman
School Video News
http://www.schoolvideonews.com

Diane Conklin
Complete Marketing Systems
http://www.completemarketingsystems.com

EntrepreneurLead.com
http://entrepreneurlead.com

Fidelity Investments
https://www.fidelity.com

Corine La Font
The Self-Publishing Center
Between the Lines: Empowering Network
http://www.helpdeskja.com
http://www.blogtalkradio.com/empoweringnetwork

Melody L. Friberg
Writing and Consulting Services
http://www.mlfribergwriting.com

Marsha Friedman
The PR Insider
http://marshafriedman.com

Cecelia Haddad
Marketing Elements Pty Ltd
http://marketingelements.com.au

Adrianne Marie Hall
Anthurium Publishing, LLC
http://www.anthuriumpublishing.com

Steve Harrison
Quantum Leap Publicity and Marketing
http://www.steveharrison.com

Leanne Hoagland-Smith
Executive Coaching
http://processspecialist.com/increasesales

Insightly
https://www.insightly.com

Danny Iny
Firepole Marketing
http://www.firepolemarketing.com

Anthony Kirlew
Imagine WOW!
AKA Internet Marketing
http://www.AnthonyKirlew.com

MailChimp
http://www.mailchimp.com

Jennifer Martin
Zest Business Consulting
http://www.ZestBusinessConsulting.com
http://www.BusinessConsultingOjai.com

Marti Masterson
Masterson Insurance Agency
http://www.mastersonalliance.com.

Lana McAra
Busy Bees Unlimited, LLC
BusyBeesUnlimited.com

Garrett Mehrguth
Directive Consulting
http://www.directiveconsulting.com

Mint
https://www.mint.com

Deirdre Morhet
BASC Expertise
http://www.bascexpertise.com

PR Web
http://www.prweb.com

Joel Peterson
Pintoresco Advisors
http://www.pintorescoadvisors.com

Quill
http://www.quill.com

Psycho Tactics
http://www.psychotactics.com

Radio Guest List
http://www.radioguestlist.com

Flo Selfman
http://www.iwosc.org
http://www.wordsalamode.com

Talk Zone
http://www.talkzone.com

Technorati
http://www.technorati.com

Christine E. Till
The Marketing Mentress
http://www.marketingmentress.com

Trailblaze
http://trailblazeinc.com

Michelle Tupy
Ghostwriting, Blogging, Freelance Writing
http://www.michelletupy.com

Matthew Tynan, Attorney at Law
Pelosi Wolf Effron & Spates
http://www.pwes.com

Steven S. Tyre, CPA
The Tyre Agency
http://tyretax.com

Vanguard Investments
http://www.vanguard.com

John Leo Weber
Geek Powered Studios
http://www.geekpoweredstudios.com

Mandy Wildman
Monetize Your Vision
http://www.MandyWildman.com

Tony Wilkins
Small Business Forum Radio
http://www.blogtalkradio.com/tonywilkins

WordPress
https://wordpress.com

GOVERNMENT ENTITIES AND BUSINESS ASSOCIATIONS

HM Revenue and Customs
http://www.hmrc.gov.uk
U.K. tax issues, business start-up tips, resources and publications, and free webinars

National Association for the Self-Employed
http://www.nase.org
Everything in a nutshell to start, run and grow a small business

National Association of Women Business Owners
http://www.nawbo.org
A professional community of female entrepreneurs

National Business Administration
http://www.nationalbusiness.org
Providing resources, benefits and expert advice

National Federation of Independent Business
http://www.nfib.com
America's leading small business association

Service Corps of Retired Executives (SCORE)
http://www.score.org
A non-profit association providing counseling and mentoring programs

Small Business California
http://www.smallbusinesscalifornia.org
Nonpartisan business advocacy organization responsive to
the needs and well being of California small businesses

Small Business Exchange
http://www.sbeinc.com/index.cfm
Information and outreach center, free conferences,
marketing assistance, and publications

Startup Nation
http://www.startupnation.com
Online small business community offering free advice on
technology, funding and grants

U.S. Chamber of Commerce
https://www.uschamber.com
News, advocacy and legislative issues affecting businesses of
all sizes

MAGAZINES AND NEWSLETTERS

Business Know-How
http://www.businessknowhow.com
Small business strategies and fresh ideas

Carol Roth's Newsletter
http://www.carolroth.com
Straightforward business advice for entrepreneurs

Creative and Cultural Skills
http://ccskills.org.uk/
A U.K. newsletter related to cultural and creative industries,
events, funding and sponsorships

Entrepreneur
http://www.entrepreneur.com
Starting and growing a successful business

Family Business Magazine
http://familybusinessmagazine.com
Articles, blogs and resources for family-owned companies

Home Business Magazine
http://www.homebusinessmag.com
Start-ups, marketing, e-biz and business plan tips

Marketing Profs
http://www.marketingprofs.com/newsletters/marketing/small-business
Real world education for modern marketers

Small Business Forum Magazine
http://joom.ag/OmuX
Savvy tips on promoting, marketing, selling and working with the media

Small Business Trends
http://smallbiztrends.com/smallbusinesstrends-newsletter
Internet and social media trends, technology developments and product reviews

The Small Business Advocate Newsletter
http://www.smallbusinessadvocate.com/newsletter
Articles, blogs, videos and inspiration

U.S. Bank Small Business Newsletter
https://www.usbank.com/cgi_w/cfm/small_business/small_business_newsletter.cfm
Tips and insights on products and services to help your business save money

CONTRIBUTOR BIOS

Wendy Anderson owns WOW! Event Productions. In addition to client events, she produced the Cherry Blossom Festival SoCal (60,000 attendees) and the White Satin Wedding Show at Santa Anita Racetrack. She's on the Board of the Pasadena Chamber of Commerce, and a member of Pasadena Rotary Club and IFEA. http://www.woweventproductions.com.

Jeanette Chasworth (ASID) aka "The Color Whisperer" is a designer, author, speaker, and loves to educate people about the power of color and design in their lives. Learn more at http://www.thecolorwhisperer.com.

John Churchman is creator/publisher of School Video News (http://www.schoolvideonews.com), an online TV/Film Production resource for teachers and administrators. In previous lives, he owned an advertising/marketing/consulting firm, was V.P. of Sales/Marketing for a leading software company, was a U.K. and South Africa commercial pilot, and owned/ operated a roller rink.

Diane Conklin, President and Founder of Complete Marketing Systems (http://www.completemarketingsystems.com), is an internationally known author, entrepreneur, coach, consultant, and speaker. She's a direct response marketing expert specializing in showing small business owners how to integrate their online/offline marketing strategies, media and methods to get maximum results from their marketing dollars.

Magda de Berg, a successful online business entrepreneur based in Australia, is the founder and owner of http://www.toyuniverse.com.au, http://www.mypetuniverse.com.au and http://www.funbrands.com.au. She is passionate about promoting success and professionalism in online business.

Jan Dunlap is the Minnesota author of *Saved by Gracie* and the *Birder Murder Mystery* series. An accomplished speaker and insightful writer, she hones her humorous edge as a guest blogger on various writing, marketing, and spirituality sites. She entertains visitors at http://jandunlap.com.

Corine La Font is a self-publishing, online marketing and virtual events consultant and specialist. She is also an author, columnist, online radio host and award-winning publishing resource in the 2012 Small Business Book Awards. Find out more and get to know Corine at http://www.helpdeskja.com.

Melody L. Friberg owns her own consulting and writing services business in Northern California. In addition to writing grant proposals for nonprofit organizations, she dedicates time to animal rescue and welfare efforts, especially for disabled cats and rescued German Shepherds. http://www.mlfribergwriting.com.

Isabel "Liz" Green has a Ph.D. in Psychology from Claremont Graduate University. She has worked both in Los Angeles County and in private mental health clinics and has been in solo practice for more than 20 years. She has had extensive experience with testing and evaluations and specializes in assessment, diagnosis, and counseling of children, adolescents, and adults. http://www.isabelgreen.com.

Cecelia Haddad's expertise lies in developing a long-term vision and strategy for clients with inherent consideration of the bottom line. She has been advising and training executives for many years and focuses on assisting them to become the expert, whether presenting to a small audience, large group or on camera. http://www.marketingelements.com.au.

Scott G. Hauge is President/Founder of Small Business California, a non-profit, non-partisan advocacy and education group for small business in California. (http://www.smallbusinesscalifornia.org). He is also President/Owner of CAL Insurance and Associates, Inc., (http://www.cal-insure.com), serves on 20+ boards, commissions and committees throughout San Francisco, and is Vice Chair of the California Commission on Disability Access.

After spending 30 plus years honing her skill set for business management, customer service, and organizational development, Adrianne Marie Hall embarked in 2013 on a long-awaited entrepreneurial endeavor when she started Anthurium Publishing LLC, an independent publishing house "Where Writers Become Published Authors". Learn more at http://www.anthuriumpublishing.com

Dianne Harris is an award-winning artist and design maven, noted Australian and French Quarterite style-setter, solo entrepreneur, truth teller, community activist, grainy retro video actress and CEO of tour de force eclectic boutique Oonkas Boonkas.You can find out more at http://www.oonkasboonkas.com and on Facebook and Twitter.

Leanne Hoagland-Smith works with solo entrepreneurs to answer this question: Are you where you want to be? With 30 years of practical business experience, she coaches, speaks and writes to quickly multiply results for people and businesses. http://processspecialist.com/increasesales

Mindy Littman Holland was the sole proprietor of Littman & Associates, a marketing communications and public relations business, for 20+ years. Today, she is an author, photographer, artist and blogger. For more information, visit http://mindylittmanholland.com.

Danny Iny, a.k.a. the "Freddy Krueger of Blogging," is the proud founder of Firepole Marketing. He's also the author of *Engagement from Scratch!, The Naked Marketing Manifesto*, and *The Audience Business Masterclass.*
http://www.firepolemarketing.com.

Anthony Kirlew is an entrepreneur and digital marketing expert who has helped countless companies and organizations improve their online presence, generate leads online, and increase revenues. Anthony is Co-Founder of

Imagine WOW! and Founder of AKA Internet Marketing. He's also a contributor to *Media Magnetism*. Learn more at http://www.AnthonyKirlew.com.

Jennifer Martin is a published author, business coach, and the founder of Zest Business Consulting. For more than 15 years she has helped small business owners, managers, and leaders get out of overwhelm and build thriving businesses while enjoying balanced, meaningful and soul-satisfying lives. http://www.ZestBusinessConsulting.com and http://www.BusinessConsultingOjai.com

Marti Masterson established Masterson Insurance Agency in October 1996 in Northwest Indiana. She is a leader who believes in being an active member of the community and sits on various boards including United Way of Porter County and Housing Opportunities. She is also an active Rotarian. http://www.mastersonalliance.com.

Lana McAra is an award-winning author of 20 titles with more than half a million books sold writing under the name Rosey Dow. She's an owner of Busy Bees Unlimited, LLC, a Digital Marketing Development company specializing in social media, email broadcasting, blogging, and telesummit facilitation. Learn more at BusyBeesUnlimited.com.

Garrett Mehrguth, is the President and CEO of Directive Consulting. Directive Consulting is located in Orange County, CA and specializes in digital consulting, developing, and marketing for small to medium size businesses. Garrett has his degree in Economics and his Masters in Business Administration. http://directiveconsulting.com

Deirdre Morhet, founder of BASC Expertise, has developed a sharp eye for how businesses get bloated with inefficiencies, specifically when it comes to cash flow and taxes, and how they can retool for a sleeker, smoother, strategically focused organization. http://www.bascexpertise.com.

Sarah O'Bryan brought her design studio to life in 2002. Twelve years later – with a thriving business and three little superheroes in tow, her book – *Business and Baby at Home -*

covers what type of business to start, creating an original brand, making money, achieving goals and managing work/life balance. http://au.linkedin.com/pub/sarah-o-bryan/15/533/662

Joel Peterson is CEO, Pintoresco Advisors, a consulting firm (http://www.pintorescoadvisors.com). Concurrently, he is Founder and CEO, Student Planning Services, an educational services company. He's been a senior executive with AT&T, British Telecom, BellSouth and a VP with U.S. and international banks. Mr. Peterson served seven years as a U.S. Navy officer.

With a Bachelor Degree in Industrial Design, Emilia Rossi co-owned a high-end fashion boutique and an online store. In addition, she co-owns two online businesses: http://www.emiliarossi.com.au and http://www.capriess.com.au. When she's not blogging, she reads up on the latest digital marketing news and helps others realize their online marketing potential.

Flo Selfman is a public relations consultant for books, authors and live events; proofreader-copy editor for manuscripts, business materials and web copy; and president of Independent Writers of Southern California (www.iwosc.org) since 2003. A longtime often home-based sole proprietor, Flo knows the value of in-person networking. www.wordsalamode.com

Shari Stauch, creator of Where Writers Win, has been involved in publishing and marketing for 30 years, first for individual athletes, and now for authorpreneurs. She speaks at conferences around the country on practical methods of online author marketing. The WWW team's mission is to "shrink the web" for authors. http://www.writerswin.com.

Christine Till, author of *Fired at Fifty: Stop Looking For Work and Discover What You Were Meant To Do*, has 20+ years of marketing background. As a science major with business management and accounting, she brings to today's modern business theater a wealth of knowledge, experience and expertise as "The Marketing Mentress." http://www.marketingmentress.com.

Michelle Tupy (http://www.michelletupy.com) is a
ghostwriter who quite happily spends most of her time
behind the scenes writing blog posts, articles, e-books and
Facebook commentary on behalf of busy entrepreneurs.
Currently based in Cusco, Peru with her family, Michelle is
in the process of researching her next working destination.

Matthew Tynan (Pelosi Wolf Effron & Spates) is a
transactional attorney specializing in the preparation of
intellectual property and corporate agreements and the
protection of client copyrights and trademarks. He earned
his J.D. from the Benjamin N. Cardoza School of Law and
received his undergraduate degree from Oxford University.
http://www.pwes.com

Steven S. Tyre has been a CPA in the Los Angeles, CA area
since 1974. He formerly worked for the international
accounting firm of Coopers & Lybrand before starting his
own practice specializing in taxes, estates, trusts and small
businesses. He shares offices with his son, Tony Tyre, a tax
and estate attorney. http://tyretax.com.

John Leo Weber is Head of SEO for Geek Powered Studios
in Austin TX. As a serial entrepreneur he has helped to
launch and develop dozens of businesses across the country.
He is passionate about helping others fulfill their dreams of
business ownership through online marketing efforts.
http://www.geekpoweredstudios.com.

Mandy Wildman is known as 'the slightly psychic success
coach' because her spirit guides offer assistance during
mentoring sessions. Mandy's worked with soul-centered
solopreneurs for more than 15 years. She lives with her
family in the mountains of Western North Carolina and can
be contacted via her website at
http://www.MandyWildman.com.

Tony Wilkins is the host of Small Business Forum Radio
(www.blogtalkradio.com/tonywilkins) and the Editor- in-
Chief of Foodie Quarterly and Small Business Forum
Magazine available at http://joom.ag/OmuX .

Ben Yennie is Co-Founder of Producer Foundry and Founder/CEO of Ben Yennie and Associates LLC, an independent producers' representation company. He is also author of *The Guerilla Rep: AFM Success on No Budget.* His background is with the Institute for International Film Finance, and more details can be found at http://about.me/benyennie.

MEDIA MAGNETISM:
HOW TO ATTRACT THE FAVORABLE PUBLICITY YOU WANT AND DESERVE

Is your business close-up in perfect focus?

Attracting – and maximizing – great PR opportunities for you, your idea and your organization is as much an art as it is a science if you want to sparkle in today's competitive spotlight.

Media Magnetism: How to Attract the Favorable Publicity You Want and Deserve is a must-have resource covering all aspects of modern media relations. Over two dozen industry experts offer insider tips, resources and guidelines on how to:

- Make influential connections
- Become sound-bite savvy
- Endear yourself to reporters
- Survive awkward moments
- Use social media wisely
- Manage a cost-effective campaign

Looking for that portal to media magic? This edition is available in paperback and Kindle at Amazon.com and Barnes and Noble. A supplemental website (http://mediamagnetism.org) features guest blogs from experts around the world. If you'd like to share your own experience and advice as a business owner, we'd love to hear from you!

www.ingramcontent.com/pod-product-compliance
Lightning Source LLC
Chambersburg PA
CBHW021424170526
45164CB00001B/83